The Needy and the Neglected in Developing Societies.

Zacchaeus Ogunnika
and
Joyce Moody Edwards

Order this book online at www.trafford.com
or email orders@trafford.com

Most Trafford titles are also available at major online book retailers.

Print information available on the last page.

ISBN: 978-1-4907-7143-4 (sc)
ISBN: 978-1-4907-7145-8 (hc)
ISBN: 978-1-4907-7144-1 (e)

Library of Congress Control Number: 2016904225

Trafford rev. 09/22/2016

 www.trafford.com

North America & international
toll-free: 1 888 232 4444 (USA & Canada)
fax: 812 355 4082

CONTENTS

ACKNOWLEDGMENTS

The Needy and the Neglected in our Hostile Society

Many individuals, intellectuals, and groups contributed a lot to the success of this book. It will be impossible to acknowledge all of them by name.

Our gratitude goes first to the subject of the book, the units of analysis, who are the needy and neglected. We acknowledge them because their observation fired our motivation to analyze their plight and try to see the failure of perspectives that our discipline, sociology, has been following to explain their harrowed experience in this society. Their patience, endurance, and reactions to the pseudoacademic character assassination of some of these analyses also needs commendation. Our attempt to understand what was responsible for their resilience in face of this abject poor condition was responsible for the ideas in this book.

We thank our Creator for giving g us good health and the ability to complete this book. Our thanks go to our students in such courses as Sociological Theories, Social Stratification, African American Experience, Sociology of Developing Societies, Rural Sociology, Social Problems, and Marriage and Family. The inquisitive nature of these students concerning global and United States social structure affected the production of the book. We, however, relied heavily on the neglected at the underdeveloped society based on the imitational approach sold to such countries from the West. We believe one can understand the plight of the needy and the neglected from the West if we can analyze the results of the exportation of the ideology of neglection to these nations from the West.

The book benefited a lot from works of experts on the needy and neglected from developing societies. We acknowledge president Kwame Nkrumah of Ghana, Julius Nyerere of Tanzania, chief Obafemi Awolowo and Namdi Azikiwe of Nigeria, and the like for their ideas shown in practice as politicians and leaders and in their writings as intellectuals. We owe a lot to some intellectuals who became the voice of the neglected. In this group are Walter Rodney, Akin Mabogunje, Patrick Wilmot, and Aaron Gana.

Our big thanks go to the affected, the depended variables of this book who are the poor, the homeless, the urban slum dwellers, those who are disproportionately affected by the criminal justice system, the aged and the sick, and the laborer working and earning below poverty line. This book is aptly dedicated to them.

Our thanks go to our colleagues in the department whose friendly relations created an environment friendly for academic development. We were particularly indebted to Dr. M. Hossain, Dr. Hogson, Dr. G. Ahmed, and S. Spencer for their support. We are thankful to Ms. Grisell Campbell for her administrative assistance.

Some of our students need to be specially mentioned for their inquisitive and thought-provoking questions, especially in the Social Stratification and Sociology of Developing Societies, Rural Sociology, and African American Experience courses: Marlene Brown, Woods, Anthony Jackson, Nike Okegbenro, Brenda White, Tomecca Perry, Asia Frazier, and Ebony Mitchel.

Our thanks go to the members of our families who supported us by coping with the shortage of quality family life during the production of this book.

We hope you will enjoy reading the book and also give us your constructive criticisms, which will advance the course of the development of knowledge in this field. Lastly, we accept the responsibility for all the shortcomings of this book.

Petersburg, Virginia
June 5, 2016

Zacchaeus Ogunnika
Joyce M. Edwards

CHAPTER ONE

The Problems of Coordination and Control in Women's Community Development Programs

Introduction

Increased complexity of functions of an organization necessitates the activity commonly referred to as coordination.

Coordination is a key word that helps an organization to survive. This is true of Women in Development (WID) organizations in our societies today., An organization becomes complex if its activities manifest into several programs that require specific but different areas of expertise and expert ideas to actualize. These different programs are regarded as part of a common whole, and their purpose is to achieve the general goal. It will then be foolhardy for the management of an organization to allow the different programs to pursue their different goals without cooperating with one another. Such an action is referred to as irrational because it lacks coordination, and surely, the central goal will be difficult to attain.

In some organizations, the various subgoals necessitate the division of the whole organization into departments, all of them working toward the attainment of the central goal of the organization. This results in what is called a complex organization because of the differentiation into departments that had occurred within the department. In such a case, there is a great need for coordination in the organization. In sum, the central ingredient for any organization's success is the effective coordination of the activities geared toward the central goal of the organization. The ability possessed by different managements of different organizations toward effective internal coordination marks the difference between the success and failure of organizations.

Coordination activities are particularly important in a women's development organization because its programs are geared toward women's enlightenment. One of the major aims is to make women become active participants in their own and their society's affairs so that their contributions to economic development will be understood and acknowledged.

This goal is central and unique, but the activities required to achieve the goal are numerous. First of all, the WID program needs to exist, and existence means that there must be adequate resources and investments to back it up. To achieve this goal, the WID program should generate funds. The program therefore needs to engage in fund-raising activities. Fund-raising activities also need coordination because there are different types of fund-raising exercises that can be achieved with different methods. The overall activities need to be coordinated effectively in order to produce results.

Apart from fund raising, WID goals include the emancipation of women from the shackles of ignorance and poverty. This means that women need to be educated and made aware of their problems through awareness campaigns and women's education programs. Women need to be trained to have skills to ensure their independence. Women need to develop leadership skills through training. It is through adaptation that energy is obtained from the environment for the upkeep of the organization. An organization usually lines up activities to aid it in its adaptation process, but these activities alone cannot keep organizations going. They need to be coordinated with other activities in the organization for the realization of the total goal of the organization. For WID programs, adaptation requires that fund raising has to be harmonized with other activities

The second problem a successful organization should confront is goal attainment. Parsons explains that adaptation is important, but it will only end up in the planning stage if there are no activities geared toward the achievement of the goal of the organization. In most organizations, this function is seen as political. It is political in the sense that it relates to the ability of the organization to effectively utilize power to get what it wants from the environment. In case of WID programs, the goal-attainment function relates to how the activities of the various women's institutional and noninstitutional organizations are coordinated in order to acquire the needed resources—how the various women's development organizations (such as Family Support, Women in Nigeria [WIN], and other organizations) coordinate and relate to the source of power to get what they want. Without a proper goal-attainment activity, the WID program will be adversely affected. But as the theme of this chapter says, no function can, by itself alone, achieve the goal of the WID without coordination with other functions.

The third function is integration, which is a system of rewards and punishments for the organization members. This function is based on the premise that all cannot always be smooth within activities and people in an organization. Some individuals are more zealous than others, while some are criminally minded, while some are really doing their work. There must then be a system of rewards and punishments to integrate the different elements. If there is no integration system in an organization, then there will be anarchy, and everybody will be doing what he likes. To achieve this function, rules and regulations—usually referred to as organizational formalization—are instituted to guide the behavior of members. This can be noticed in the WID program rules and regulations.

Lastly, the pattern must be maintained by settling new entrants into the system. This function refers to how members are recruited to the organization.

This is very crucial to the coordination of the WID program. It refers to how the program gets its new converts among women and even men, young and old, in society. If patterns are not maintained, then the organization may cease to exist in due course. This activity in WID requires various propaganda, awareness campaigns, and training (including workshops, conferences and seminars) to acquaint people with its programs. By doing so, the pattern will be maintained.

In discussing the theoretical explanations, it is discovered that each of the systemic problems is very important, but it cannot stand on its own. If the organization concentrates alone on anyone without adequately coordinating all of them together, it will be difficult for the organization to achieve its goal. This underscores the importance of coordination and control in the WID program in Nigeria. As explained in this paper, each of the systemic problems constitutes a project for the WID, but none should be given more attention than the others in order not to make it become the only focus of the organization. Fund raising is important from the adaptation side, but trainings and workshops to develop the women and make them come out of poverty is also very important. This necessitates the coordination of the activities for effective harmonization and goal attainment.

Ingredients of Coordinating Activities

The activities involved in coordination can be enumerated in order to understand the ingredients involved. In other words, what are the contents of a coordinating action, and what should a coordinator of the WID program be working for? The activities involved in coordination are the following:

An entity. Usually called the organization.
Goal. The purpose for which the organization is set up
     initially.

Strategy. The actual tactics, and activities involved in the
    achievement of the goal.

Planning. This precedes the strategy and is a major activity
    of the coordination that leads to the coordinating
    activity.

Human activities. Aimed at a strategy to achieve the goals.

The projects. Each of the specific objectives turned into
    action, which is observable at particular times.

Monitoring and evaluation. This is the activity of the
    coordinator or the coordinating body at a self-
    reevaluation of past activities to assure whether the
    activities are yielding results or a change of action
    and direction are necessary.

The Coordinating Agency

In the generic sense, *agency* refers to "the actor who
causes the occurrence of an event or an action." In the
language of statisticians, *agency* is referred to as the
independent variable, while the event that was caused by
the agency is a dependent variable. In the case of WID
programs, the coordinating agents are the independent
variables as they make the event—coordination—occur.

Two major kinds of coordination systems—an
individual acting alone or a coordinating agency—
have been identified. When coordination of activities
in an organization is being done by an individual, the
organization is said to be highly centralized. If it is in a
committee comprising of people in the organization from
all levels, then authority is decentralized. It is even more

decentralized if coordination is done in stages according to the different hierarchies and levels of the organization.

Both of these systems can be analyzed in order to identify their usefulness or otherwise for women's development programs. An individual as coordinating agent is useful when the activity to be coordinated is located in one place. The coordinator should be highly knowledgeable in the form of activity in question. This form of coordination must be surpassed by the kind of rules and regulations referred to as maximal formalization. Authority in such a situation is said to be highly centralized.

Coordination by a single individual has its advantages. First, decision making is very fast as there is no need for long meetings of policy makers. He makes his decision based on his expertise and his understanding of the cultural and political environment. Second, there will be no internal squabble and rancor among the policy makers since he is the only person. The enforcement is also fast, as he can supervise it himself.

This agency has its own disadvantage, especially in a complex organization. If diverse knowledge is necessary, the sole coordinator becomes a liability. His knowledge alone cannot carry the day. He may also make a lot of mistakes without advice. If the human variable is highly heterogeneous, his presence might bring trouble, as the people may allege an accusation of sectionalism, especially by those who are from his own section (race, class, or ethic group).

The committee agency is the second possibility. In this case, the coordination is a group of people who act together.

Each member of the committee may even have a special area to coordinate. This kind of agency has the advantage in the sense that a decision will itself be more accurate. There is the advantage of the minimization of errors in the sense that each contributes his knowledge and expertise.

In a heterogeneous organization, it may serve as mechanism of tension management as the groups might be able to identify their own members in the committee. The disadvantage is in the sense of very long processes of decision making, as there can be disagreement in the committee meeting. It is also vulnerable to committee internal conflict, which affects the coordination activity. In case of the WID, we believe that a committee system is desirable, as it will take care of the heterogeneous nature of Nigeria.

The Process of Coordination

There are three major processes of coordinating human activities leading to the effectiveness in organizations such as the WID. These are the autocratic, the supportive, and the laissez-faire approaches.

The approaches refer to how a human agent actually operates in the coordinating process.

Coordination is laissez-faire when the coordinator allows all the variables being coordinated to do what they, in their own opinion, consider as good and correct. He does not give orders and does not even show leadership by example. On their own, the people take shapes without a shepherd. This kind of agency has been criticized as inadequate. It has been concluded that the organization under him might not achieve the goal. More studies show that human beings need to be directed in order to work. Eric Fromm has also documented the danger involved when man is given what he calls "too much freedom." He will certainly misuse it.

The autocratic approach is the opposite of the laissez-fair. Such an agency believes that people must be forced to work. Coordination of activities are done without the ideas or advice of those that are being coordinated. The agency decides the projects, strategies, and actions without consulting the beneficiaries, which in case of WID programs are the Nigerian women.

This approach was referred to by Batten as the "directive approach." In criticizing such an approach, Batten said that the nondirective approach is better. This is a situation whereby the beneficiaries themselves are contacted before or on the coordinating activity.

The autocratic approach in coordination creates alienation and frustration in those being coordinated and also within the beneficiaries. Some schools of thought argue, however, that this approach is situational. In occasions where people are not enlightened and unaware of their rights, this approach seems to be the best.

The supportive approach is the one whereby coordination is participatory. The agent acts as a primus inter pares. He is a leader but not a boss. He has a love of his job and believes in the welfare of his workers and those being coordinated. The program to be designed is due in consultation with the beneficiaries and not for them but by them. Researches also showed that the supportive agent will achieve a goal result.

Conclusion and Recommendations

This chapter has looked at the issue of the coordination of the Women's Development Programs. It was concluded that coordination is very important, as it is through the activities that the goal of women's emancipation, empowerment, and poverty alleviation can be achieved. The goals strategy, and human activities involved in the WID programs need to be harmonized and coordinated. Similarly, the different projects are all geared toward the achievement of the central goal enumerated earlier. These different projects relating to poverty alleviation, fundraising training, and workshop and awareness campaigns also need to be coordinated.

It is also affirmed that coordination can be through the committee or individual system. The process can also be autocratic and supportive.

On the basis of all these, the following recommendations are put forward as a means to effective coordination of WID programs.

There must frequent monitoring and evaluation of the WID programs to ensure their being in the right direction. Obsolete ones should always be dropped.

There should always be researches so that programs will not be obsolete. In the end, I recommend that a department of research and development (R and D) should be established to help the process of coordination.

The committee system should be adopted in view of the diverse nature of Nigerian women. This will ensure a conflict-free atmosphere for effective coordination of WID programs in Nigeria.

There must be good publicity, and communication should be accorded a central place so that the objectives of the WID would not be misunderstood.

CHAPTER TWO

Principles and Methods of Vocational Guidance and Selective Placement for the Disabled

Introduction

This chapter describes the principles on which vocational guidance is based and attempts an examination of the methods of selective placement in order to determine their efficiency and stimulate thought, which will generate ideas toward positive innovation.

In order to achieve this, the chapter will explain the major variables, take a look at the theoretical foundations, and examine the principles and methods involved in the issue of vocational guidance and selective placement of the disabled in our society. We will conclude with an attempt at an evaluation of innovations meant to improve the present methods and principles of vocational guidance and selective placement.

Definitions

This chapter is addressing management or organizations practitioners whose function is to help change the condition of the disabled to what is desired by helping them realize and accept the best vocation suitable for them and also who will place them in a type of job in which they best fit. The chapter is therefore meant for helping professionals who are engaged in the human services of helping humanity. One of the best imperatives of man in order to survive is adaptation to the environment. Adaptation, Talcott Parsons says, is the ability of organisms to acquire resources from the environment for their own use and survival. This process is called work (Ogunnika 1984, Hydebrand 1977). Work, however, is not just something out there ready to be done. To perform work meaningfully, one needs to possess a skill that will help the actor in the adaptation process. Work is not just a random process whereby a person just wakes up being able to do anything. It is a result of the interconnections of the society as everybody in society cannot be doing the same thing. If such a situation happens, adaptation will not be possible. To solve the problem of maladaptation of human beings in society, a process called division of labor emerged (Durkheim, Smith). This is a process that recognizes the special abilities of individuals and encourages each individual to develop to the fullest the areas where he is best. The process requires a man to develop that skill that his physical condition allows him to. Productivity will increase if everybody can perform the jobs for which they are fitted based upon their physical condition (Taylor).

One of the imperatives of man is to find the best activity that will allow him to adapt to the environment. This process is called *vocational choosing*. It is, however, believed that inhabitants of the deep (fish) do not recognize water. Similarly, in most cases, the individual may not know the activity to which he is best suited. This happens because one might not understand his biology or his social environment. In such a case, he needs to be guided to the vocation necessary for his adaptation. This process is referred to as *vocational guidance*. It is performed by vocational guidance counselors in schools and other development and corrective institutions such as remand homes, prisons, and rehabilitation centers. These kinds of workers (those who take care of disadvantaged people) are called *helping professionals*. To do this work, they themselves need to acquire a lot of skills and be literate in some subject areas, which include occupational psychology, sociology of occupations and professions, and social work. They also need the knowledge of industrial engineering and industrial relations. All these will help them grasp the skills and strategies to correctly guide recipients. The strategies gained from their knowledge in this area, which is actually utilized to guide people, is referred to as methods of vocational guidance.

While the philosophy behind the guidance is called the principle of vocational guidance, selection and placement is the actual fitting of a man into the job where he can best perform by utilizing his acquired vocation. Selective placement, in the ideal situation, refers to the competitive and qualitative putting of a worker on a job by considering the level of his attainment as far as a vocation is concerned.

It particularly refers to the act of fitting an individual into the job that his vocation shows he can perform best. The major principle of selective placement is the prevention of placing a round peg into a square hole. It helps eliminate placing an individual into a situation where he will not be productive. In one word, in selective placement, an individual is put in the job he can do best based on his vocational training.

Theoretical Background

The subject of this chapter has arrested the attention of both the classical and contemporary thinkers (Smith, Taylor, Parsons). I will, however, analyze the best known, least admired, but mostly practiced of such theories—the scientific management of Frederick Taylor.

Prior to Taylor's submission, Adam Smith's theory had laid the foundation for selective placement. He was the one who said that in doing a particular job, the tasks should be separated into parts, which should be divided among individuals to ensure highest cooperative productivity. Though this theory did not specifically refer to vocational specialization, it nevertheless addressed the issue of division of labor, which is the major principle behind occupational specialization. Smith's theory informs the issue of vocational specialization because the main principle behind it is the increased work productivity to help man's adaptations to his environment. It may even be added that Smith believes that an individual should do the work he can do best in such a division of labor.

This theory is extended to a very large extent by Frederick Taylor in scientific management or taylorism. His major contention in the theory is that human beings are different in their ability and are capable of doing different things. They cannot fit into the same job. He wants vocation (if I may say) to be scientifically designed, and we should scientifically chose people for these different vocations.

Taylor could be called the first theorist to discuss the principle and method of vocational guidance and selective placement. His ideal is that scientific knowledge should be utilized to select individuals for the types of work they can possibly perform. This has now resulted in some of the principles of recruitment and job placement. It has also infiltrated into the methods of vocational guidance and selective placements today.

Principles and Methods

The major principle behind vocational guidance and selective placement is adaptation to the environment. By this we mean many things and at many levels. Adaptation is the ability for one to influence his environment so that he could acquire the resources required for his survival. This process is what is commonly called work, and an individual, in the process of adaptation works on his environment in order to get the best out of it. The environment may be economic, social, scientific, cultural, academic, and the like. The principle of vocational guidance states that an individual should be studied and guided as to which of these areas he is fit to work. He is there to engage in vocational usefulness to the areas from where he gets his daily bread. Adaptation, the principle believes, is at different levels:

1. The individual level
2. The community level
3. The larger social level

If there is no vocational guidance, individuals will just get to wrong vocations where they become liabilities and useless to their society. It is believed that if a majority of individuals get proper adaptation, this will help the community they belong to adapt. An aggregation of adaptation by the community will definitely help the larger society. Vocational guidance therefore helps the individual discover himself and supply his best for his own benefit and the benefit of the society. To achieve this lofty aim, one needs to use appropriate methods for the guidance of the individuals.

The earliest methods utilized some personality clues for vocational guidance and job placement. This includes what is known as tests of ability, intelligence quotient (IQ) tests, and personal observation and interviewing.

These methods are deficient because they are only oriented toward the personality and not trying to uncover the interrelationship between the person, his environment, and the larger society. It has been found that a person's intelligence quotient is not static. It is a variable that can therefore grow and the size of the IQ depends on the society where the observed lives. To test the IQ of a person at a single point in time and conclude that he should be placed on a vocation leading to a certain job will lead to mistakes. Vocational guidance should be projection should look into the future and the past. In trying to guide a subject, a kind of regression analysis is necessary. We should uncover all the past elements of the respondent's life and use them as predictive tools to our expectation of his development in future. This one will help us to place the respondents into the appropriate vocation without a larger chance of error. The society where the recipient will also work is an important ingredient to be considered in vocational placement. He should be prepared for a society where he can successfully mesh without a problem. A good vocational guidance should also be recipient oriented. By this we mean that we have to supply the data of alternative vocation and the type of placement they lead to, to the recipient. He should be the last to choose the vocation based on his interest. This method brings results as it has allowed the actor to discover himself.

Most vocational guidance methods follow what Ogunnika (1989) referred to as meritocratic, which implies a counselor or an authority administering a test to the candidates. Various cutoff points are arbitrarily created and particular vocations are attached to each of the cutoff points. A person is then fixed to a job based on this arbitrary cutoff point. This method has been seen to have a lot of problems. It has been described as discriminatory, elitist, and inconsiderate of human variations. The argument is that we believe that to use one universal test to assess the readiness of all individuals' future success in vocation suffers from too much overgeneralization. Secondly, personality differences and community orientation are not taken into consideration by such tests. That is why we have a lot of failures in products of such selective placements. Evidence has shown that we discover more motivation and commitment among apprentices who chose their own vocation and were permitted to do it by themselves. Most of our local tailors, mechanics, and painters have been more successful than some who went to the arts and crafts schools by means of selective examination.

A good vocational guidance method should be based on the following principles.

1. It should be oriented to make the recipient useful.
2. It should alleviate poverty at the individual, organizational, and community levels.
3. It should reduce crime (since those who could have been unemployed will be gainfully employed).
4. It should get the beggars and the destitute out of the streets.
5. It should increase the overall productivity of the society.
6. It should serve as an avenue for helping professionals perform their human services for the benefit of society.

Conclusion

Vocational guidance and selective placement is very important in the society. Looking through its principle, it is the avenue through which one can alleviate poverty, crime and delinquency. If it is also properly done, the whole society will benefit, as productivity will increase. The chapter, however, concludes that certain methods, especially the one that is meritocratic, may not help yield the desired result. The vocational guidance method should not only be personalty oriented, it should be organization and community oriented. The areas of the society's needs and the person's ability should be given a meeting point. This is to forestall a situation in which a vocational trainee will not have the choice of placement in order to be useful, a vocational specialist should have the opportunity of being placed to work in the society. We need to make a census of the areas of need in society, identify the vocations required, and then find the personalities that will be distributed into the various vocations in the areas of need in the society.

CHAPTER THREE

Placement and Aftercare Resettlement Services of the Disabled in Nigerian Communities

Introduction

The economic trends in the world today make it imperative for a country to try to reduce the number of its dependent population. Individuals, whatever their health conditions, age, and capability, should be encouraged to be productive toward the national economy. The antipoverty dictum is that one must try to produce at least what will sustain him. The national surplus is, therefore, the aggregate requirements left over after an individual has produced what will sustain him.

This fact was behind most government policies in the third world, and it underscores the importance of placement and aftercare service resettlement of the disabled. The mere fact that a person is incapacitated and disabled does not mean that such a person should be a beggar and should depend on the charity or the goodwill of other individuals forever. A disabled person is not displaced nor eliminated from productivity, especially after rehabilitation. The only effect of disability on a disabled person is to force him to develop a change in capability. For example a person who has been a good footballer before an accident that caused him to get an amputation might have his capacity to play football removed, but it does not prevent him from being a good analyst of football for the consumption of the lovers of the sport.

Here disability has changed his capacity and such a person should be placed accordingly. His contribution to the general economy will therefore still stay. His football column in a newspaper might be the main attraction to the public who reads the paper. The main aim of rehabilitation is therefore the discovery of this alternative capacity after the original has been taken away by the trauma or anything that has caused the disability.

This chapter is, therefore, stressing that a rehabilitated individual should be resettled and be placed in a workplace, as he can be as useful as any worker. The practice of discriminating against rehabilitated persons in workplace should be stopped, as it is against the fundamental human rights of the disabled and also militates against quick economic recovery in this country.

Approaches to the Disabled Issue

Approaches to the issue of the handicapped or the disabled have some difficulties because most definitions failed to grasp the problem and a few others cannot explain the whole variance in the situation. The definitions vary and range from the extreme legal or statutory, through the academic/ or intellectual, to the unique (as seen by the affected).

Legal or Statutory

The statutory or legal approach should be seen only as classificatory. Disability is divided into categories, which include the mild, moderate, severe and profound categories. The mild categories include the blind, the deaf, the educational subnormal, and the partially blind and deaf. The severe categories include the epileptic, the physically handicapped, and those with speech defects (Davies 1979, 136). According to this definition, disability can be further categorized by gender (male, female) and age. Hence, one can talk of handicapped children. The law under fundamental human rights provides that they should not be discriminated against on the basis of their disability. This is the major flaw we got from the statutory definition. It is easy to declare that a handicapped has the right to get anything, but how will this right be transferred to reality? This question also shows the importance of the rehabilitation and placement of the disabled. Only when the disabled is physically rehabilitated and actually placed can one conclude that law recognizes the existence of a disabled. No employer will definitely employ a disabled who has not been rehabilitated. Statutory classification of disability has also run into another problem, especially when dealing with disabled children. On this, Davies said

> Considerable criticism has been leveled at these (statutory categories which are not necessarily related to the needs of the children and which tend to emphasize separate education in all instances and give no indication of multiple handicaps (i.e. child recommendation to abolish statutory categorization and to replace it with a recorded system of educational need.

(Davis 1979,136)

In short the legal definition of disability has failed to explain the whole variance. The major point of rehabilitation and placement is left out. This is expressly seen in the Nigerian Constitution of 1989, which was never used. Chapter 4, section 32–44 expressly provide for the fundamental human rights. No section specifically touched on the rights of the handicapped nor their replacement and rehabilitation. Section 41, which specifically provided for the right to freedom from discrimination, was only general and not specific on the plight of the disabled. The provides that a Nigerian citizen shall not be subjected to discrimination on the basis of creed, sex, birth, place of origin, religion, or political opinion. It is very important to note that the word *disability* is absent.

Academic Approach

This also has its own flaw. By its use of superior logic, it is suffering from what Horkeimer (1977) calls the *eclipse of reason*. The academic definition is not so sure about who is disabled. This is due to the consideration of what it called the agency. By this, it is meant, who is to be accused as the cause of the problem?

As we shall elaborate later, this led into the emergence of the two schools of thought on the disabled which has a serious consequence on the need to rehabilitate and place the disabled.

The academic definition distinguishes between disability caused by the society itself by a process called labeling, and the one that occurs naturally whereby the sufferer cannot meaningfully participate in the activities that will lead to a goal of the society. Mental disability is the first group, while physical disability caused by a physical disorder through accidents, chemical change in the body, or hormonal deficiency caused by external agents such as viruses and bacteria are the example of the second group. According to Szasz (1961) there is nothing like a mental disability or illness. It is myth. What is applicable is and erroneously labeled as mental illness are only the problems of living.

Mental illness is, therefore, a label placed upon certain deviant behaviors exhibited by certain individuals. It is very wrong for such people, because they are not disabled at the onset. Theirs is a deviant behavior occasioned by the problems of life and not sickness. Such is the confusion in the academic definition of the handicapped that it almost became handicapped and disabled in itself in an effort to contribute to the problem of the disabled.

The Actors' Side Approach

This approach is based on the dictum that "he who wears the shoes knows where it pinches." The approach believes that only a disabled can define his disability. If a person's hand is cut, or he is epileptic or blind, but he believes that he is not disabled and can get his daily bread all by himself, then he is not disabled. An individual is not supposed to be addressed as "disabled" or treated as such unless he submits himself for such a treatment. This approach has an important ally in some theoretical or ideological movements in social thought.

The first school of thought is what is called the ideographic approach, which seeks to understand phenomenon from the actor's side. It believes that events can only be explained by those experiencing them. Outsiders who are not part of the experience can only describe what they see, but will not understand nor grasp the real truth behind events and issues. The issue of disability, their rehabilitation, and placement can be understood by the disabled. The legal and academic approaches can only describe and produce a copy of the truth. The production of large statistics and array of logic which are the products of these two earlier approaches may not help one to understand the problem of the disabled.

Instead they will deceive us and make us not understand the problem.

The second intellectual foundation of this approach is ethnomethodology. Ethnomethodology frowns at what it calls the influence of external rationality in human behavior. It says the only rationality that should be allowed to guide a behavior is the rationality of the actor himself. Any other observer from the outside will create irrationality. It particularly criticizes the academic approach, which it believes is glorifying itself in emptiness. The expert in the situation of rehabilitation is the one who has experienced it, and it is his own account, which cannot be faulted. To grasp the importance of placement and resettlement of the disabled, one needs to turn to the disabled himself according to this approach.

Theoretical Foundation

There are two theoretical foundations to the issue of the disabled and destitute, each of them explaining and prescribing what is to be done. The first approach, known as the conservative approach, believes that the disabled are the causes of their own problems and should not be helped. The second approach, which is the progressive approach, believes that the disabled are the problems of society; they are less privileged and, therefore, should be helped. The first approach is supported by evolutionary theory, which manifested in the modern-day functionalist approach. It based its argument on the principle of survival of the fittest, having got the blessings of such academic giants such as Spencer, Durkheim, and Talcott Parsons. The main arguments are that the disabled need not be placed nor rehabilitated. The world is a place where human beings must necessarily struggle for survival. This struggle, according to the functionalist, is for the development of the society. It is therefore very wrong for any government or organization to bring a policy that will not allow such a struggle to manifest. The aggregate world development will suffer if some population has to depend on others for their well-being. All must be producing for the general well-being of the society. We should allow destitute and the disabled to be deselected so that life will be better for the remaining people in the society. The disabled constitute a danger to the ongoing development of the society.

This approach saw no importance in the rehabilitation and placement of the disabled. In fact they, according to Herbert Spencer, should be allowed to die off.

It is this approach that informed the action of people who propagated the ideology of eugenics, who were trying to create a superior human race for the betterment of humanity. Those who are like the disabled in the world should be allowed to die off.

The above approach was squarely attacked by the progressive, who stressed the importance of the rehabilitation and placement of the destitute. According to them, a disabled was placed in the position he is because of society's situation. Some are too poor to take care of themselves before their position became so bad.

Most of them became what they are, not because that they lacked ability, but owing to lack of opportunity. He approach believes that society has two groups: the haves and the have-nots. The approach utilizing the influence of Marxian dialectics submitted that the haves forcibly arrogated all the opportunities of the society to themselves, which eventually created the disabled both mentally and physically. To create equity and fair play in the society, the disabled should be rehabilitated and be placed. To this school of thought, one of the most importances of the placement of the disabled is for social equity and fair-play. The approach also believes that society will be better off if this subsector (the disabled) is taken care of as a conflict management mechanism by creating social harmony, which is a prerequisite for economic development.

In summary, the two approaches highlighted the rehabilitation and the placement of the disabled. The conservatives believe that there is little or no importance in it, as it will cause social underdevelopment, but the progressive believe that it must be done. We shall now examine the state of the art it is in our society today.

Rehabilitation Placement and Aftercare Service

Rehabilitation is a practice whereby the disabled, in whatever form, is given a kind of treatment to enhance the following:

a. To make the disabled physically or mentally fit to operate in the society.
b. To create in him an alternative skill, especially if the nature of his disability has destroyed his original skill.

c. If his disability is congenital, to create in him
   a situation not to make him totally useless to the
   society and a mere dependent.

This process involves both medical treatments and
training. The medical practitioners attack the source of the
disability in order to create a physiological condition that
can be helped by training. Training, on the other hand,
involves the inculcating the disabled with skills for creating
useful products or services.

In most cases, the two processes are simultaneous. In
some cases, the training aspect of rehabilitation cannot
be embarked upon until the disabled is physiologically all
right. The time the disabled is undergoing rehabilitation is
called the care time.

Placement and resettlement denotes the act of actually
fitting the disabled into a particular sphere of the social
system—usually in an organization—for the purpose of
his engaging in productive activity. This is to enable him
to sustain himself and not to join the army of beggars
parading on our streets. In fact, this is another importance
of placement and resettlement of the disabled.

Problem of the Process of Rehabilitation in Nigeria

The process of rehabilitation of the disabled in Nigeria
has not received enough attention. This conclusion is based
on the points that follow.

The number of rehabilitation centers in the country is too small for the perceived number of Nigerians that need rehabilitation. In fact, there are six established vocational rehabilitation centers since the fourth National Development Plan. These centers are far too small for the country.

The vocational rehabilitation centers are even poorly funded, and their establishment seems not to be based on any strong empirical research. We believe that these centers should be situated all over Nigeria, with one in each state of the federation. The handicapped and disabled are funded everywhere. We believe they can be placed in areas where some kind of disabled care is shown. That is, we should try to make the activities of the vocational centers agree with local and cultural conditions.

i. It is unfortunate that rehabilitation is defined in Nigeria as only vocational. Rehabilitation should be total, and the result should be able to equip the recipient to function normally in the society. In most developed countries, rehabilitation and placement affect all aspects of life. In Britain, for the disabled to live a meaningful life, numerous acts were enacted, which include the Chronically Sick and Disabled Persons Act 1970. The act gives special responsibilities to local authorities in respect of those who are substantially and permanently disabled (Davies 1979).

It provides for their enumeration, provision of services, and types of help available. In fact, housing authorities should provide certain things in the house to make it accessible to some kind of the disabled. Viewed in this form, rehabilitation and placement should not be only vocational.

To be properly resettled after services, the society must ensure that some conditions not favorable to the disabled are taken care of. For example, there should be a smooth staircase that can be used by disabled person on a wheelchair.

A mentally disordered person just rehabilitated must not be put in a situation where agitation will worsen his condition and cause a relapse in his condition.

Nigeria lacked a strong legislation to aid rehabilitation and resettlement after the care services for patients. The laws available are not even well enforced.

ii. The ministry responsible for social services under which the schedule for rehabilitation and resettlement fall are very handicapped legally and human resources–wise. In fact, they are not formally sound to do their work.

Most organizations are not ready to employ a rehabilitated disabled. This is even evident in the statement on the Nigeria First Rolling Plan published by the ministry of budget in 1990. The objective of rehabilitation is to make the disabled get some skills and be self-employed. This is easier said than done. Most of these disabled are left to poverty after being discharged from these rehabilitation homes. Laws should be enforced to make organizations employ the disabled, as it is being done in other countries, especially in

Britain, where a certain percentage of the workers of an organization should be rehabilitated disabled workers.

Importance of Placement and Aftercare Service Resettlement

Despite its numerous problems, the importance of the placement of disabled after rehabilitation cannot be overemphasized. As mentioned earlier, the benefits realized from that one according to the individual disabled and the society at large. The importance can also be looked at in an institutional way because it has economic, cultural, and political implications.

Consider first, the importance to the individual is great. If a disabled is not rehabilitated and placed, he becomes a burden to some people. Mostly, these people might not be financially well enough to support him. The next thing is that he transfers the burden to the society by becoming destitute and a beggar. This is what experts refer to as "the journey from disability to destitute." Such a journey kills the personal confidence in the disabled and adds more to his problems. In fact, it results in multiple disabilities.

For instance, a disabled who knows that, despite his disability, he still possess some skills that are not allowed to manifest because of nonresettlement or nonplacement might become a mentally disordered case. Most of the beggars on the street would have not been there if they had been resettled or placed. The motivator's theorists, especially the social psychologists, agree that one of the inherent attributes of man is to be in a situation where he can obtain his self-actualization. The disabled are also human beings, and they have aspirations and personal goals. Placement and resettlement will make them achieve this actualization. In saying this, one can remember Stevie Wonder, the blind artist, and Gary Coleman the artist boy with a kidney problem. In biological terms, both are disabled, but in actuality, they have been well-placed and achieved even better than normal individuals.

Most of us are witness to the wonders being performed by the vision impaired and those who are hard in hearing (deaf and dumb). They create artwork, and some of them have even successfully sat for and passed examinations up to degree levels. If such people are discriminated against by not being well resettled, it will give them a psychological problem.

In summary, resettlement of the disabled is very important at the individual level, as it makes them feel part of society and it helps them in achieving their self-actualization.

At the society level, the importance can be considered in a generic form and also institutionally. In the generic form, one of the goals of most governments is to get beggars off our streets. The solution to the problems has been likened by this author to cutting off a banana tree from the top in order to destroy it. Any casual observer knows that this will not work as the banana will always grow again. Most governments have been removing the beggars (most of whom are disabled) and keeping them in a place (sometimes rehabilitation centers).

These beggars are poorly taught some trades and are left to go and become self-employed. The truth, however, is that immediately after they leave, the beggar goes back to the streets again. Here lies the importance of placement and aftercare resettlement of the disabled. The beggars in our streets will only be reduced if, after rehabilitation, they are placed appropriately and resettled.

Institutionally, the importance of placement and resettlement of the disabled has an economic dimension. The disabled will be able to contribute their quota to the economic development of the nation rather than being only a dependent. If well managed, the rehabilitation homes can aim at sustaining themselves utilizing their products and still produce surplus for the society. Individual disabled who are well-placed will be contributing to the welfare of others. A large dependent population will not help a nation achieve economic prosperity.

Politically, if disabled are well-placed, it will enhance the human rights image of the nation in the eyes of others. In fact, some other nations will be taking examples from this nation. This will be a big political development. The placement and resettlement of disabled can even achieve internal reconciliation politically. This happened early in this century in America. In a case in court, it was established that a case of discrimination can be established if evidence can be led to show that a race or ethnic group has a larger proportion of its members in a group being discriminated against. Similarly, if disabled are not well-placed, and a group, clan, or ethnicity can prove that most of these disabled belong to it, then it amounts to discrimination. Such national crises will be averted and interethnic, interclass, and interstate harmony will create if the disabled are rehabilitated and resettled. In this form the action will serve as a mechanism of intergroup tension mechanism management in Nigeria.

Conclusion and Recommendation

This chapter has attempted a review and an analysis of rehabilitation and resettlement of the disabled generally, with particular attention to the problem envisaged for developing societies especially Nigeria.

Disability, this paper says, should not be allowed to become inability. We should create ability from the disability by developing alternative skills and abilities for the disabled. This, the paper believes, can happen through rehabilitation. Resettlement and placement are considered by this paper as the horse that rehabilitation will ride to achieve its goal. This is the major importance of placement and resettlement as discovered by this author. Rehabilitation and care of the disabled without placement will produce a result as if the disabled has not been rehabilitated at the outset. In addition, we have seen the resettlement of the disabled and their placement as a potent agent of national economic development, positive and harmonious international political propaganda, and potent mechanism of intergroup tension management.

We, however, believe that while placement and resettlement are very important, of no less importance is rehabilitation itself. If the process of the care of the disabled and the rehabilitation is not well-done, then the placement and resettlement will not be possible. To this end, the following recommendations are made:

The process of rehabilitation and care of the disabled in Nigeria needs some improvement. We believe the improvement will be possible, especially now that women's ministry and social services issues are put together. As women, the impact of the problem will be well grasped, especially in relation to disabled children and women. It is recommended that the ministry should move an awareness campaign to alert the public of the importance of rehabilitation of the disabled.

NGOs (nongovernmental organizations), charity organizations, affluent individuals, and other organizations should participate in rehabilitation and resettlement of the disabled. The situation whereby the government is left alone to take care of the disabled is not normal.

In Britain, several laws were enacted to force the public to come to the aid of the disabled. As far back as 1944, the Disabled Persons (Employment) Act was passed. These acts maintain their census and specially make the provision for their placement by stating that "every employer who has twenty or more persons on his staff must always employ a minimum of 3% disabled persons." This is very encouraging because it is being enforced. In Nigeria, such laws—if even existing as covered by our fundamental rights of freedom from discrimination—is hardly being enforced.

Instead, the placement of the disabled in Nigeria is being jeopardized by the effect of dangerous cultural beliefs and stereotypes about some kind of disability. Such problems are not only affecting the disabled but are also affecting their families. For example, some employers believe that mental disorders, epilepsy, and the like are hereditary. They are not only refusing to employ a rehabilitated sufferer upon a lot of campaign and popular workshops plus publication of books to feed the public with the correct idea on the importance of placement and resettlement.

Resettlement should recognize Nigerian culture. Nigerians are unlike Europeans, a people who do not subscribe to the idea of "possessive individualism." The disabled can therefore be settled together in their own colony. Affluent persons can create disabled factories where the workers will all be disabled and produce for market and their own sustenance. In fact, they will help the national economy in so doing.

Government, especially, in developing countries should also liaise with the departments of special education, sociology, economics, and law in the universities to assist in the rehabilitation. Disabled children and even adults need counseling on career guidance. Some have congenital disabilities, and others have lost their skill and need to be counseled on new ones. This fact is well captured in Britain where the training service division and employment service division are established to cater for rehabilitation and placement of the disabled. Rehabilitated disabled are employed in what is called the open industry, which is like any ordinary occupation. Here, the disabled compete with others, and the shielded employment which a government subsidized full-time employment. This paper recommends that Nigeria should adopt both policies in order not to lose the contributions of the disabled to the general economic development.

The total focus should not only be toward making the disabled self-employed. Some of them need to work to get enough money in order to establish their own job. In that case, they will not be depending on anybody.

CHAPTER FOUR

Bridging the Sociocultural Communication Gap between Patients and Health Providers for Effective Community Development

Organizational effectiveness has been seen by experts to be a function of communications. Executives and organizational members including their clients will be unable to understand themselves if communication is not effective.

C. I. Bernard (1956) says that communication is the backbone of effectiveness of the function of the organizational executives. Effectiveness suffers when impediments are allowed to make smooth communication impossible. Smooth communication is required within the members of an organization horizontally and hierarchically. It will enable the members to comprehend the activities leading to the goal of the organization and contributes to the identification of the goal itself. Similarly, effective communication is necessary between organizational members and their clients. This fact is well spelled out by Robert Katz and Daniel Khan in their analysis of organization as an open system. It is believed that inability to communicate with the environment of the organization will result in misunderstanding of the organization by the clients, which will eventually result in less energetic input (i.e., loss of revenue, sales, or patronage) to the organization.

The hospital as an organization consists of health providers, who are the doctors, the nurses, the pharmacists, and the paramedics. This group most necessarily interacts with patients. For treatment to be effective, a thorough communication is required between these health providers and their clients, that is, the patients. Once communication is ineffective between them, the whole function of the hospital will be impaired. There are many things that might lead to ineffective communication, but none is as dangerous as the one based on the sociocultural gap. If the sociocultural gap is not bridged between the health providers and health seekers, communication between them will be distorted and the goal of the hospital will be displaced and unattainable.

The main focus of this chapter is the identification of the sociocultural impediment to effective communication in health organizations and how they can be effectively controlled.

Communications and the Problems of Distortion

Communication is said to be the dynamic aspect of organization. Ginsberg (1972) asserts that communication is essentially a social process because it is through it that contact is established between mind and mind. This is what he calls intersubjectivity—whereby an actor can establish the thought of the mind of the other. At this behavioral stage, if the contact is well established, there will be a good understanding of the other actor. Unless the ego understands the alter or the actor, the two interactants cannot meaningfully achieve the goal in question. This means that communication is not effective. The health seeker (patient) and the health service worker must put themselves in a situation that will allow their two minds to settle on the same thing. It is only when this happens that the goal they both see care of the patient will be achieved. The two minds of the patient and that of the health seeker can only meet if there is effective communication.

Effective communication is, however, a function of many things, bordering on sociocultural factors. The presence and absence of these factors (such as language, belief system, types of education, and the like) affect the intersubjective understanding of both the clients (patients) and the health service workers.

The elements in the communication process are all functions of sociocultural conditions. The process includes the sender, the medium, the message, and the receiver. A communication is said to be ineffective if the message sent cannot be received by the receiver. This might be due to many things. Communication contains information or data meant for the use of the receiver to effect an action. The goal is the action. Whenever the action expected by the receiver is not due, then the communication is ineffective. A receiver may become a sender and vice versa. This is what is referred to as two-way communication. This is the situation in the hospital. The patients communicate with the health workers, and they, in turn, communicate with the patients. The care for the patients becomes very effective if this process is not interrupted. In most cases, the process of communication is always aborted, is incomplete, or ends up in confusion. Experts call such a process communication distortion (Habermas, Ogunnika 1993).

Communication distortion is very bad for effective care of the patient. It may cost discomfort for the patient, and it has been leading to losses of life. It also leads to psychological torture for the health worker. Literature is replete with the agony of health service workers who reported helplessness when their patients are faced with severe pain and sometimes avoidable death. Such a condition, the health workers assert, occurred because such patients are those whom they cannot understand or who could not understand them owing to imperfect communication.

Communication distortion is a function of many things. It may happen if the sender is not well equipped to send the message in an intelligible language to the sender. In such a case, we talk of a faulty medium. The receiver may also not be equipped to understand. The medium may not be available to both the sender and receiver. Both of them (sender and receiver) might lack a common medium for the communication. The medium may even not be available. All analysis of the statement above show the importance of socioeconomic factor especially in the health sector. A doctor acting as a sender may not be effective to his patient if he is not knowledgable in the client's type of illness, especially if he could not say the truth because of a cultural condition. In fact, some cultures believe that an educated man like a doctor is omniscient. Such a doctor may not say the truth to the patient. This becomes incomplete and distorted communication and makes the patient suffer. A patient sometimes may not understand and force himself to agree owing to cultural dictates of not showing ignorance.

In fact, researchers have shown that a respondent or a patient who sees his status as lower than that of the doctor will not communicate well, for he will always be laboring to satisfy the superior person, even if it means doing the wrong thing.

Communication, especially at the interpersonal level, such as that between the patients and the health service worker is basically interpersonal. It therefore depends mostly on the understanding of the interactants, sociocultural conditions.

At this level (between patient and health workers), communication is essentially carried out by the sociocultural properties of symbols, signs, language (spoken and silent), and the like. This gives this kind of communication the status of a spiritual operation by which patients and health workers transact their business of life, which may be spiritual or material (Ginsberg 1972). It is essentially an exercise involving silent language that can only be comprehended by understanding sociocultural conditions (Hall 1973, Ogunnika 1982).

Any gap in sociocultural understanding between the patients and the health workers will certainly place a great difficulty on communication and consequently affect the quality of the patient's care.

Sociocultural conditions are those imperatives that aid our comprehension of the environment found within various societies. One can be acquainted with them, either by being a member of such a society or by the process of socialization. Sociocultural imperatives manifest themselves in education, technology, belief system, socioeconomic status, religion, family orientation, geographical background of the actors (rural or urban origin), and ethnicity or racial affiliation. Sociocultural conditions vary. It possesses the variance between and variance within. The variance within is the degree of differences in sociocultural conditions between different categories in the same society. Different categories include class, occupational group dispersion in space of individuals according to socioeconomic condition. The variance between refers to the degree of difference in cultural imperatives between members of one society and the other based on their understanding of their various environments.

The sociocultural gap that affects effective communication is therefore a function of these variances. Individuals from any cluster or group manifesting these differences will definitely find it hard to understand themselves on issues. Such a situation may kill their efforts at arriving at a common definition of a goal. In case of the health care in hospitals, it will create a misunderstanding between the patient and the health workers.

Once the health workers and their patients are speaking in different languages, the quality of patient care suffers. That is why this author believes that the sociocultural gap existing between the patients and the health service workers need not be too wide, and if it is wide, it needs to be bridged for effective patient care.

Elements of Sociocultural Gap

In this section, we shall examine the elements of sociocultural gap that manifests in the within and between variances noted above and result into ineffective communication between patients / health service workers.

Health institutions in Nigeria are divided into categories—the primary, secondary and the tertiary institutions. The sociocultural gap between patient and health service workers varies between these health institutions as the table below shows.

Types of institutions	Within	Between
Primary	+++	+
Secondary	++	++
Tertiary	+	+++

Source-Created by the author

Table 1 above shows the sources of sociocultural gap variances in communication between patients and workers in health institution. The table is based on the demographic composition of the clients and the workers. A good understanding of the table will help in finding the solution to the gap which is a major cause of in effectiveness in patient care in health institutions.

Primary Health Institution

According to the table, primary health institutions have the majority of variances in sociocultural gaps within the society where it is situated. This is based on the object of primary health care and the demographic composition of the interactions. Primary health-care institutions serve the grassroots. Patients are those from the immediate local environment. Most of the health workers (nurses, paramedics, etc.) are from the local environment. The sociocultural gap between these workers and their patients result from differences which are found within them.

According to table 1, most variances are within with a very few between variances. The between variances are result of some of the health workers from other societies who might be working in the localities of a few strangers in the society.

Primary health institutions are found mostly in rural areas. According to Robert Redfield, the distributing feature of the rural area is homogeneity. It was said that rural societies are small, isolated, and homogenous. Despite this, there is still a sociocultural gap between the clients and the workers. Such a gap is always acquired through socialization, and they consist of what the individuals themselves achieve, such as education and wealth. Belief in non-African religions such as Islam and Christianity also accounts for such differences. This can be well comprehended in table 2 below.

	Elements
1. Primary	Education, socioeconomic status, religion/ family orientation
2. Secondary	Ethnicity/race, geographical background (rural or urban), education, socioeconomic status, religion/belief system.
3. Tertiary	Technology, occupation, race/ethic, geographical background, religion/belief system, education, class/ economic status.

Table 2

The primary health institution is largely preventive. It works by advising the clients on what to do prevent health hazards and the treatment of minor ailments and accidents in the numerous clinics provide. This sector is the most important if one goes by the Alma-Ata Declaration. If sickness is nipped in the bud, health for all in the years ahead will be possible. Sociocultural gap in the rural areas seems to be preventing this.

Bisi Ogunnika (1994) has opined that some individuals still believe in the ancient theory that diseases are caused by evil spirits. She went further that such a people believe that such spirits should appeased. Most of the objects utilized to appease these are themselves health hazards because they are not hygienic. This group of people is unable to comprehend the advice of health workers based on the sociocultural elements mentioned in table 2. Education constitutes the source of the variance between the clients and health workers in these rural environments. The gap becomes wider since the socioeconomic status of the educated is enhanced by his job in these small villages. The health worker and his client are therefore unable to have effective communication. This has led to numerous deaths and discomforts for these rural patients. In some cases, differences in acquired religion and family orientation create problems. Those in the Islamic and Christian religion will not necessarily believe in the ancient theory if diseases are caused by spirits. This will contradict those still holding this belief. Family orientation of the village health workers is always different from those of the clients. Although there is no hard statistic to support it at present, it is, however, believed that health workers in the villages are from liberal homes that are receptive to innovations and new ideas. This constitutes a gap in communication between them and their clients.

The secondary health institutions are curative hospitals. As table 2 shows, all the elements causing ineffective communication in the primary institutions are present with its own additional ones. Here the variances are both within and between as table 1 shows patients coming to these hospitals are from both local environments and farther off. They (secondary health institutions) serve a larger geographical spread than the primary health institutions. For the variances within, the socioeconomic status here assumes a higher dimension because the understanding of inferiority and superiority is actually more pronounced. There are gaps between the patients themselves as some with higher socioeconomic statuses are accorded more respect. They are placed in private rooms and eat better diets. This creates a big gap within the patients and between the patients and health service workers.

Geographical backgrounds of patients and workers manifesting in either rural or urban orientation is an important factor of sociocultural gap in secondary and tertiary health institutions. These factors reinforce the belief system of the patients and affect their health seeking habits. It also explains a lot of variances in faith in the hospital. People from urban backgrounds might be more used to the hospital. The health workers and patients from urban areas at least possess a common variable, being urban, which might aid communication between them. However, a patient from rural settings in the hospital might not comprehend the actions of the doctor. Ethic and race orientations also constitute a gap. In most hospitals, the health workers (especially the senior ones, such as doctors) are not from the ethnic groups of the society where they are serving. Some of these workers are not even from the race of the patients. This constitutes a serious sociocultural gap in fact this becomes a bigger problem if the conception of illness and health-seeking behavior differ between the ethnic or racial group of the patient and worker.

They will be operating at different levels and might not have faith in themselves.

In the tertiary institutions such as teaching and specialist hospitals, patients are referred from the lower health institutions. The demographic compositions of such hospitals are mixed. Sociocultural gap is mostly felt here.

Communication gap is affected by the various occupational gaps of the patients, ethnic orientation, education, religion and most especially class orientation. The element causing the gap, which is substantially different from that of the secondary and primary unit, is the technology. The technology in the tertiary hospital is highly sophisticated and may constitute a sociocultural gap between patients and workers. The patients, whatever their backgrounds, may be new to this machine and cannot comprehend them. Some may even fear the techniques, such as the tests and surgical operations in the hospitals. Until the patients are made to understand this, it might be difficult to give them good care. This is based on the fact that one will definitely not enjoy what one has comprehended.

Bridging the Sociocultural Gap

Effective communication will be possible if the sociocultural gap is bridged. This should be done at the three levels of health-care delivery systems, so that the customers and health service workers will understand themselves.

At the primary health-care level, the gap is mostly caused by the within differences. The people should have been homogenous had it not been for the influence of the external variable that appeared to differentiate them. The variable that differentiated the people and created the sociocultural gap was education, which was externally propelled. It created the gap between the health workers who received it, thereby modifying their stand on the cultural belief system. The acceptance of education also raised the recipients' socioeconomic status and affected the family orientation. To bridge a sociocultural gap in the primary health-care level, it logically follows that the externally propelled variable, education, should be made to reach everybody. If this is done, the cumulative effect will be on everybody in society and improve the communication process between the customer and health-care workers. Primary health-care clinics should go along with adult literacy campaigns. There should be mass mobilization of awareness, whereby the society members will be taught the benefit principles' characteristics and the benefits of health institutions. The relationship of this to the traditional health delivery system and even religion-based therapy should be analyzed.

Rural-urban differences found between the customers and practitioners can also cause problems, especially in secondary and tertiary levels. The rural man is supposed to be fatalistic, remote and isolated from the mainstream of things. This is based on the fact that the rural areas have been suffering neglect. The rural man is always a different man, especially at secondary health institutions where his outlook to life is different. He is poor, unable to pay for the treatment, and sometimes might not understand why he should even go for the treatment. To bridge the sociocultural communication gap based on rural-urban differences, the level of neglect of the rural areas needs to change. Education is not only acquired from the classroom. One acquired education from the experiences gained from the environment. If the necessities of life are provided in the rural areas, the rural dwellers will be conversant with those things that made him unable to comprehend the communication with the man of urban experience. The rural is too far from the urban in terms of socio experience.

If the rural neglect is well arrested and popular education in the rural areas is geared up, communication problems in the hospitals based on rural-urban sociocultural gap will be reduced and the quality of patient care will improve.

In addition, the health service workers need to show examples if the sociocultural gap is to be bridged. One of the problems confronting patient care is their (rural dwellers) lack of trust in the imported health-care system. A belief system that says spirits should be appeased in order for one to be healthy is rampant in the minds of most patients.

This belief must be removed for effective patient care. We have witnessed patients leaving the hospital to seek health with *babalawo* or the *malams*. Their belief is however reinformed by the attitude of some health workers who engage in the same practice. It confirms patients' belief when they meet nurses, doctors, and the like in the same *malam* clinic seeking for the same care.

The health-care workers spoke a different language in the hospital and another outside the hospital premises. This makes the patient lose faith in the hospital service and increases the sociocultural communication gap. It shows that the health workers themselves doubt the bases of the health-care technology that is used for things like medical tests and the numerous surgical operations. Patients with this kind of experience will not understand the language of such a technology and will also refuse it. They will rather say that such a medical health system is not meant for them since even the health service workers themselves have refused to use the hospitals.

In all, this paper has argued that a sociocultural communication gap exists in the health-care system in this country. It needs to be bridged in order bring effective patient care. Its bridging is a work of proper socialization of the society and the provision of essential things, especially in the rural areas to bring the rural dwellers nearer to their urban counterparts. Finally, the health workers themselves must demonstrate their faith in the health-care system by patronizing the modern hospitals.

CHAPTER FIVE

Renewable and Sustainable Alternative Energy Sources and the Issue of Women's Development in Third-World Communities

Introduction

It has dawned on the world population today that the total health of mankind is highly dependent on how available energy is used and the possibility of discovering sustainable and renewable energy sources.

An alarming fact that was recently established (1985) is that the survival of our planet itself depends on how we can wisely utilize energy. In the same vein, the various sources of energy have bestowed mixed blessings on the locations they were found in. It has bestowed wealth on Saudi Arabia. In Nigeria, Petroleum has brought mixed blessings such as the economic development of the oil boom of 1970s while at the same time contributed to rural neglect and decay. It eventually caused the Nigerian civil war of early 1970s and the Nigerian Cameroons conflict over Bakassi.

This chapter is concerned with an aspect of energy that is very important today. It has been established that this planet cannot continue in existence once the source of energy has been depleted. The question that arises is "What can we do to prevent the depletion of our sources of energy? How can we extend the lives of energy sources are using now? How can we produce alternative sources of energy that are not only an alternatives but renewable developments in the area of alternative source of energy.

In most societies women were not properly consulted on the issue of energy, especially in the developing societies. However the issue of energy affects men and women equally, we can argue that women are more affected than men being the nearest to the children and home maker. If energy is removed from home, then homemaking becomes impossible. Researchers have shown that 75 percent of energy consumed in most third world societies is made of fuel—wood utilized and consumed in the home by third world women. It has been established that this source of energy is now causing problems for the environment, especially in the Sudan-sahelian region. Fuelwood as energy source encourages desertification and other environmental vices. This shows that a debate on finding alternative renewable energy source will go a long way to help women to overcome one of their major impediments. In the subsequent section of this paper we shall do the following:

i. Take a global look at position of energy today.

ii. Understand the energy sources in the developing countries.

iii. Examine the effect of these on women and the environment.

iv. Identify the renewable energy source presently available to women and do critical view of their sustainability and

v. Examine the alternative source of renewable energy especially for third world countries.

Global Position

In this section, we shall identify the global reserves of the various types of energy sources in order to determine their availability. Energy sources can be categorized in the generic sense into two categories, which are renewable and non renewable. The fossil fuel and nuclear energy belong primarily to the nonrenewable while solar, wind, tidal power, and most biomass sources are renewable (Sarre and Smith, 1991). In terms of energy, the fossil fuels (which includes petroleum and natural gas) constitute the most frequently used in the world today. It has replaced coal as the most important ingredient energy used for industrialization. Most homes cannot operate without the use of fossil fuel for cooking, heating, and cooling. The development of the automobile greatly increased the rate at which fossil fuel (especially petroleum) is being used, and this made the countries of the North become the greatest energy consumers. This situation is adversely affecting the environment and is making the planet Earth an increasingly unsafe place for human beings. Tables 1 and 2, give an uncomfortable picture of the world reserve in fossil fuel in the world and highlight the need for the world to find alternative source of energy which will be sustainable.

Table 1

Global Proved Reserve of Petroleum (1989) in Thousand Million Barrels

	Country	Reserve	Percentage of Total
1	Middle East	660.3	65.27
2	Canada	8.3	0.82
3	Western Europe	18.4	1.82
4	USA	34.1	3.37
5	Latin America	125.2	12.38
6	Africa	58.8	18.11
7	USSR	59.9	5.92
8	Asia and Australia	46.6	4.61
	Total World Reserve	**1,011.6**	**100**

Source: Sarre and Smith, 1990. Adopted from *BP Statistical Review of World Energy*, 1990.

Table 1 reveals a point made earlier when we stated that energy determines the direction of both the world politics and economics.

In the world's petroleum supply, the dominance of the Middle East is very clear, and we could see that since 1973 the attention of the world has been directed to that part of the Middle East, which lastly ended in the Gulf War of 1990. It is in the realization of this fact that Reddish (1991) has this to say:

> Current perception of the amount of these fuels now available gives an instant image of powerful economic and political influences at work at the end of the twentieth century.

Recently, United States introduced fracking technology to increase the world's supply of oil. If approved by all parties and receive positive opinions, it will actually boost the world potential fossil fuel reserve. However, experts doubted its positive effect on our environment.

A fuel reserve that has not drawn a lot of political confusion but which has contributed a lot to environment degradation is coal.

Observation shows that use of coal as a major industrial energy source is on the decline despite the fact that historically coal was the major energy source for industrial development and even revolution in most industrialized countries. Coal has done a lot of damage to the environment before it is being replaced by oil, however oil is not better as it also adds to environmental pollution. In fact oil seems incapable of driving coal out of industrial use as and it is argued that coal has a reserve which can last for the next 1500 years while oil may not exceed the next century in existence. The bottom point is that if the search for alternative energy is not intensified now the world will be less clean and safe for we may have to go back to the use of coal again.

Table 2

Global Reserve of Natural Gas 1989 (in Trillion Cubic Meters)

Countries	Reserve	Percent of Total
Russia & Eastern Europe	43.3	39.00
Canada	2.7	2.43
Western Europe	5.4	31.26
Middle Europe	34.7	4.86
USA	4.7	4.23
Latin American	6.7	6.40
Africa	7.5	6.76
Asia and Australia	8.0	7.21
Total World Reserve	**113.0**	**100**

Source: *BP Statistical Review of World Energy 1989* Computation by the author.

Table 3

Global Reserve of Natural Gas (in Trillion Cubic Meters)

Countries	Reserve	Percent of Total
USA	261	28.49
Western Europe	78.8	8.6
USSR	239.6	26.15
Eastern Europe	89.9	9.81
Latin American	18.6	2.03
Canada	6.8	0.74
Africa	62.1	6.84
Asia	68.1	7.43
Australia	90.7	9.90
Total World Reserve	916.2	100

Source *BP Statistical Review of World Energy* 1990. Computation by the author.

Although *proved reserve* refers to those resources extractable under the present condition and not the total available, the picture is clear that fossil fuel are not renewable. This shows that the world should for alternative form of energy that would be sustainable. A sustainable source of energy is the one that will serve our present need without prejudicing or compromising the needs of the unborn future generation (the Brundtland Report, *Our Common Future*, UNO 1987). Not only are these three dominant sources of fossil fuel nonrenewable, they are also dangerous to the continuous existence of life and the environment in this planet.

Energy Source in the Developing Countries

This problem is much more for the third world, Africa, and the Sahelian region. Most of this region depends on biomass for energy especially in the home. This has a direct implication for the women because the region is not highly industrialized.

More than 50 percent of domestic energy is used in homes for cooking by the women. Experts, however, noted this hithertofore renewable biomass source of energy is no longer renewable. In fact, its continuous usage will adversely affect the lives of both man and animals. The time for trees to grow and replace the pelted ones take too long, during which the land would have been left to the unfavorable effect of desertification and, sometimes, erosion. This affects agriculture and allows the adverse effect of the harmattan to ravage the areas without any protection. This account shows that an alternative source of energy is also necessary in the developing world, especially in the Sahelian region, to save the environment. This will also save the poor women the agony of being labeled as those who degraded the environment by depleting the supply of trees utilized as fuelwood.

In fact, the development of automobiles has made most developing nations be dependent on fossil fuel. Ultramodern roads were built in these developing countries. Modern automobiles utilizing fossil fuels are driven on the ultra-modern roads available in some parts of these countries. There is even a shift from fuelwood for cooking to kerosene and Gas. Nigerian Government encourages cooking with fossil fuel, especially, in the sahelian region in order to preserve wood and com bat the menace of desertification. This shows that fossil fuel is also being used extensively in developing societies. The developing are therefore using fossil fuel at home, for transportation vehicles and industries.

This will definitely lead to the accumulation of the greenhouse gases like carbon dioxide (CO_2) and will eventually lead to global warming and climate change. Experts predicted that if we continue in the way we are, by the year 2030, we should expect a 1° C rise in mean global temperature and a 3° C rise in the year 2090. This rise will certainly be very damaging to human, animal, and plant life on this planet (Prints and Stamp 1991). All these observations lead to the fact that actions should be geared toward developing alternative source of energy in the developing nations to start industrialization.

A sad news from experts show that we have to work hard to achieve the development of sustainable energy sources in the developing nations. This is based on the fact that it was found that the energy intensity curve has the same shape for the developing and developed nations. On energy intensity, Prints and Stamp (1991) reveal the amount of energy (in equivalent metric tons of petroleum) needed to produce a given unit of gross domestic product. They (Prints and Stamp) therefore argue that during the period of initial industrialization, the amount of energy consumed increases sharply. If this is the case, the developing nation's propensity to consume energy will be very high since industrialization is still at infancy. Our argument is that we should try to start looking for alternative energy sources rather than the third world consuming fossil fuel such as petroleum and coal, which will add to global warming.

Secondly, the cost of fossil fuel is too high now especially for the non-oil-rich developing nations.

Impact of the Energy Source Available Now on Environment and Women

The cost of fossil fuel is even high for Nigeria, an oil-rich nation. Affordable alternative clean energy sources might move us forward. It was observed that Tanzania spent almost the whole 100 percent of her earnings on the importation of petroleum.

In this section, we shall examine the effect of the source of energy identified earlier on women generally and the Nigerian women in particular as it relates to their domestic activity. We shall also take another look on the effects of the existing energy sources on the environment. Table 4, below summarizes the status of existing energy sources.

Table 4

Availed Energy Sources in the Third World

Source Friendly to	Renewable or Nonrenewable Environment	Availability to Third World Women	
Petroleum	-	+	-
Biogas	+	+ (potentially)	+
Drug	+	+	+-
Fuelwood	+	+	-
Solar	+	- (absence of technology)	+
Nuclear	+-	-	-
Natural gas	-	+ (potentially)	-
Wind & Tidal	+	+ (can be available)	+
Geothermal	+	-	+-
Coal	-	+	-
Hydropower	+	-	-
Ethanol	+	-+	

(+ = renewable and - = not renewable)
Source compiled by author.

Table 4, identified 12 sources of energy used in the world. Out of the 12 sources, 9 sources were renewable. This would have been cheery news because only 3 were not renewable. The cheery become sad when a further analysis as to the intensity of usage, availability, cost per intensity, and the environmental effects of their usage are conducted. It has been established that the 9 renewable energy sources are only numerous in number but are in the minority in actual usage.

The Brundtland report on our common future shed more light on this fact. Oil, coal, and gas (the nonrenewable source) remain the big three in terms of commercial energy production and consumption. In 1984, oil accounted for 40% of the total commercial energy consumed in world while coal's share was 30.3%, followed by natural gas at 19.6%.

The above shows the total effect of the 9 renewable energy sources—in addition to the ones not mentioned here—account for only 10.1% of the total world consumption. The world will be in more danger if the proportion of consumption between the sources of energy remains in its present form. There will be a 40% increase in the consumption of fossil fuel in the year 2025. The unit utilized in measuring energy consumption is called terawatt-year (TWy)which is equivalent to one billion tons of coal. By 1980, the world consumption stood at ten terawatt-years, but by 2025, we expect to consume fourteen terawatt-years.

This will affects the sustainability of proved fossil fuel reserve and produce negative effects on world's environment as explained below. Sarre and Smith have predicted that at the 1988 level of usage oil will last for only 42 years. This did not happen because of new discoveries and even the discovery of fracking which of course is injurious to the environment.

Natural gas possesses an average of fifty-five years. Coal will last longer, and according to Prints and Smith (1991), it can last for the next 1,500 years. Even Sarre and Smith (1991) believe it will go to twenty-third century. The information here is gloomy and not encouraging. It has been established that fossil fuels are being used as the catalysts to develop all the materials of modern civilization. What happens to civilization if the source finishes? Computers are powered by electricity, which itself is produced by burning another energy source. Most of human knowledge is in the computer today. If oil dries up, will the knowledge not also vanish? This is more serious, as the other renewable sources mentioned in table 4, such as nuclear sources, have adverse effects on the environment.

Coal, which has the longest life span, is the worst, considering the effect on the environment with regard to greenhouse warming up. The conclusion from this is that the three fossil fuels cannot guarantee sustainability. Sustainable development is utilized here, following the Brundtland Report as "the development that meets the need of the present without compromising the ability of the future generations to meet their own needs." The present position of the leading fossil fuel will not generate sustainable development. This will be truer in insert of after the word consideration their total effects on the environment and man in (2) below.

Experts have agreed that not only is fossil fuel unreliable in terms of renewable characteristics, their effects are also detrimental to the future survival of this planet.

We are examining the effect of the use of fossil fuel energy on the accumulation of greenhouse gasses like

CO_2 and SO_2 (carbon dioxide and sulphur dioxide). It has been established that fossil fuel has a direct effect on their accumulation. This effect will eventually result in a 3° C increase in world temperature in the year 2090.

The Brundtland Report expatiates much on the effect of fossil fuel on the environment, especially as it relates to the climate and the survival of future generations of man. It recalled that fossil fuel burning contributes a lot to acidification of the environment and atmospheric pollution. Fossil fuel, if burnt without reservation at home, in transportation, and in industries, will surely lead to climatic change generated by the greenhouse effect of gases released into the atmosphere as earlier noted. It was noted that climatic change occurs because of increased concentration of atmospheric carbon dioxide (CO_2). The preindustrial concentration of CO_2 was only it should be 280 parts per million parts of air, by volume (ppm). The ppm increased to 340 and might rise to 560 before the year 2050.

The effect of this on the environment is the disruption of agricultural and forestry ecosystems and the flooding of lowland coastal areas. It will also marine life and food chains. This will have a socioeconomic effect, as agricultural trade will collapse. Eventually, this will affect the health of people, as food intake will drop. This is of tremendous effect to women. At the time of pregnancy, women need a lot of food to have a healthy fetus. Once the food chain is broken, women are in danger. This will also affect them as the homemakers. Once there is climatic change affecting the food, the home (which is a cherished prize of the woman) becomes the victim. In addition, the situation affects the depletion of the ozone layer, which experts say might cause a lot of health and environmental hazards. The increase in skin cancer is traced to the depletion of the ozone layer. In fact, the deadly diseases that are developing today, such as the AIDS and Ebola viruses and the mad cow disease, might be traced to the degradation of the environment by the unrestricted use of the present energy source—fossil fuel.

Status of the Renewables

The renewables, which totally amounted to about 10% of world total consumption, have not fared better. One of the most widespread renewables utilized in the world is nuclear energy. It was observed that this energy source is very useful in generating electricity.

The Brundtland Report summarized its usage thus:

> As of 1985 nuclear energy produces 65 percent of the electricity generated in France, 42 percent in the Sweden, 31 percent in West Germany, 19 percent in the USA and 13 percent in Canada. The USSR generates 10 percent of its electricity from nuclear energy. (p. 186)

This source of energy, however, has enormous problems, and it is unwise to use the source unless the unresolved problems are really faced. One of the biggest problems in utilizing nuclear energy is the threat to world peace.

Once the knowledge becomes widespread, it will lead to proliferation of nuclear weapons.

The production technique—especially using it to generate electricity—is very dangerous. This makes it almost a no-go area for the women in developing nations. Should the developing nations' governments try to go nuclear, families will be separated because the energy bill alone will consume the total family budget. This will increase the already bad situation of their debt position. Another important point is that nuclear energy is prone to nuclear accidents. The Chernobyl accident is a case in point. The problem of using nuclear energy is compounded by where to deposit the waste. Nuclear waste can cause serious damage to the environment where it is deposited. The experience in Nigeria is what no women's group would like to repeat itself. It affects the health of every organism and particularly destroys fetuses in the wombs of women. Thus, the nuclear energy might be a renewable energy source; it is, however, not in agreement with sustainable development.

Hydropower can also cause environmental problem though it is renewable. It needs a proper planning to forestall such a bad result. Methane or biogas can even produce a negative effect on environment.

In summary, available energy sources are not geared toward sustainable development in energy resources. Their effects are disastrous to the future environment. This problem is being compounded by taste, because the energy source bringing the most serious damage is the one we are consuming most in the world today as shown in table 5 below.

Table 5

Human Activities and Greenhouse Effects on Global Warming (1980)

Human Activities	Percent (%)	Gases	Percent (%)
CFCS	24	CFC	24
Forestry	18	Methane	15
Agriculture	9	Nitrous Oxide	6
Energy	46	Carbon dioxide	55

Source: Sarre and Smith 1991. Page 138, modified by the author.

Table 5 shows that human activities on greenhouse contribution is produced by energy use which invariably is fossil fuel. It shows the danger the planet earth has on overdependence on them (fossil fuel). An urgent need for alternate renewable and environmental friendly energy is necessary to save the world.

Renewable Energy Available to Women

This section will identify both friendly and nonfriendly renewable energies and examine their impacts on women and the environment. Their effects on women's domestic labor will also be scrutinized.

The foregoing analysis has also showed that the energy most frequently used is the worst for environmental sustainable development.

In fact, the oil is available to Nigerian women in the form of kerosene. However, it is a known fact that this source of energy for domestic use has two disadvantages. First, it contributes to the general CO_2 source which is bad for the environment. To prove this, all that we need to do is continue lighting our houses with a hurricane lantern without a shade. We could observe the amount of CO_2 emissions from it. The effects can be observed from the carbon deposits on the outsides of cooking pots. Secondly, kerosene is becoming unaffordable as a source of energy. Most women cannot afford it in Nigerian homes. A cleaner source of energy is cooking gas which because of its high cost in the prize charge is not affordable to poor women in developing societies. Its use is confined to the elite and better homes, and the bulk of the grassroots people cannot recognize or use a gas cooker.

The most common source of energy available to the developing country's women is biomass in terms of fuelwood. This is a form of energy that is both renewable and, at the same time, unaffordable to the women. The condition of fuelwood tells the contradictions in the energy situation which shows that a renewable source of energy might not be sustainable. Prints and Stamp referred to this scenario as the "other" (renewable) energy crisis. It was estimated that over 2 billion people which is the majority of the developing nation's population rely on fuelwood for domestic energy consumption but that over 70 per cent of them have no secure supply. The price of fuelwood is skyrocketing but at the same time the supply is dwindling. Fuelwood is renewable but the rate of consumption is far higher than the rate of renewal. The gap thus created has resulted in the environmental problem of desertification in most of the region today. The increase felling of trees resulted in severe desertification which has affected food supply chain and the health of the people. It has also been established that a large percentage of urban pollution results from burning of fuelwood. This resulted into the familiar urban smog.

In some societies, the collection of firewood dominates all daily lives. The alarming news is that half of the total wood cut in the world yearly is used for fuelwood.

Four-fifths of these are in the world's poor countries. In essence, the richer a country is, the less its consumption of wood as fuel. The insatiety resulting from the fuelwood crisis is well captured by Prints and Stamp (1991):

> The fuelwood search has bitter twists . . .
> More and more people encounter problems
> in finding wood . . . areas become
> overcut . . . [and] the trees destroyed do not
> regenerate. The removal covers opens up
> often fragile tropical soils to rain and wind
> erosion.

This is a shocking revelation. It has been established that even the burning of animal dung is not satisfactory. This is because the dung burned might have been better utilized as fertilizer for the soil of these developing nations, which are becoming less fertile because of erosion engineered by the cutting of the tress.

The account in this section, sad as it may sound, shows that fuelwood as a source of energy in the third world is as bad for the environment as the fossil fuel energy. It has a very bad effect on agriculture and human health. It also affects economic processes of women at home, as many of them spend most of their time trying to get the wood. Lastly, its efficiency is very low as gathered from the women who use it, most of whom allow more than 50 percent wastage. This also applies to the case of domestic coal at home.

The general question is then, what can we do to rid the world of energy-related environment crises? How can we help women get a more comfortable and sustainable source of energy at home? The answer to this is the concern of our concluding section on alternative sources of energy.

Sustainable Alternative Source of Energy

Our concern in this concluding section is to make cases for sustainable alternative sources of energy for the world generally and the developing world particularly. In this section, we shall be guided by Brundtland's definition of sustainable development in the report *Our Common Future* (1978). Development is sustainable if it can help the present generation achieve its needs without depriving the subsequent generation of a good living standard. A renewable energy source regeneration rate in which the generation rate lags behind the consumption rate is not sustainable. An energy source that is renewable but not affordable, accessible, and intelligible to the user population is also not sustainable.

A sustainable energy source should be one in which

i. the user can understand how it will be used,
ii. the user can afford the price,
iii. its use will not be detrimental to the environment, and
iv. it regenerates and can be reproduced as it is being used.

This definition knocks out almost all the energy sources available today. What then should be done to achieve the alternative energy sources?

Expert opinions believe that the world needs to reason and research on a sustainable development in energy. Prints and Stamp captures the situation this way:

> On the road to sustainable development we have to change both the intensity of our energy use and also the source of our primary energy supply.

Their point is that there can be a sudden change to renewable energy sources from the present. It will cost billions of dollars to set up new apparatuses even if a new energy source is developed today. One should realize the cost of changing from coal to oil in industries. The second point is that most renewable energy forms themselves are still on trial and are not yet tested on a very wide scale. Some renewables also have environmental problems. It will therefore take time for the world to sort out these problems. What will happen then before renewable energy is available? It seems that before a total change to renewable energy, we need to develop a pattern of efficient energy-use behavior. We need to make what we have now more efficient so that it will be less hazardous to society and last longer. Efficiency will surely make oil reserves last longer than the average forty-two years.

The situation should plan a transition from the present wasteful use of energy to renewable energy-use mode. Under the present system, experts submit that only one third or thereafter of coal being burned to generate electricity is wastage. In the same vein, automobile efficiency in energy use can and should be improved. In some countries, there are still automobiles burning fossil fuels at the rate of only eighteen miles per gallon. This can be increased to about fifty miles, or eighty kilometers, per gallon. It means that almost half of the fossil fuel being burned by these automobiles constitutes wastage. The same can be said of the biomass, especially fuelwood. The method utilized by the third world women encourages wastage. The stove is inefficient, and almost 65 percent of fuelwood energy constitutes wastage. We need more efficient stoves, and in this respect, Nigerian higher institutions should devise fuelwood stoves that will conserve energy. If this is done, fuelwood may return to its real status of being a renewable and sustainable energy source. The amount of fuelwood required will be reduced, and this will give time for the wood to regenerate. The Brundtland Report (p. 190) noted that there is acute fuelwood shortage in Asia and sub-Saharan Africa and that unless something is done, it will create what it calls "the other energy crisis." More than 1.3 billion people in the region utilize fuelwood.

Our point is that this planet needs a renewable energy source, but at the same, it must prolong the life and reform the pattern of usage of the present nonrenewable ones.

To this end, it has been proposed that we can utilize price to influence people's consumption pattern of fuel and the like. It has been proposed that if we add the internalized cost to the price of oil, consumption should reduce. Internalized cost is defined as things like carbon taxes or an environmental degradation tax. The revenue generated from such taxes will be utilized to extend researches on renewable energy. Nigeria has almost taken the lead in such proposal. By reducing the subsidy on petroleum, it has the Petroleum Trust Fund. A substantial part of this fund should definitely be harnessed toward researchers in sustainable energy source research and environmental cleanup. It has also been suggested that a shift from incandescent bulbs to compact fluorescent bulbs save about 75 percent electricity. This will help prolong the life of fossil fuel utilized in electric generation.

We believe that if we can conserve energy, the world will have breathing space to develop new sources of renewable and sustainable energy sources.

Renewable Energy—Solar, Geothermal, Methane, and Others

Some new sources of sustainable renewable energy seem to be what might rule the world later if given the chance to be developed. They are interesting renewable energy sources with minimal problems. They represent what is nearest to sustainable energy. These energy sources include geothermal energy, biogas, ethanol, solar energy, and wind energy.

Geothermal energy is the act of tapping the earth's natural underground heat. Thus, the use of this energy source is increasing at an average of 15 percent a year. The good thing is that its development is not restricted to developed countries alone. It is also being used in developing ones. If well utilized, it will save a lot of hard currency because this source of energy needs not be imported. It is available at the location where it will be consumed.

A Danish experiment has shown the extent to how biogas and wind energy can be utilized. Denmark produces a substantial part of the gas it uses from pig sharing using anaerobic digesters. What they did was to utilize the opportunity of what they have in plenty. Denmark is one of the world's largest exporters of pig meat (pork). Pig sharing is always available, and therefore, such an energy source is sustainable. We believe some can be done in Nigeria utilizing most rubbish, which are abundant. Our monthly clearing exercise can help supply the raw material for such an energy source.

Denmark has also developed wind turbines to generate electricity. In fact, their latest discovery can generate four hundred to five hundred kilowatts. In fact, this will be good for the northeast region, where we have constant winds blowing in the arid zone.

Conclusion

The issue of renewable energy should be considered with affordable energy. If an alternative energy is affordable but in the long run will adversely affect the economy and health of the population, then it cannot be used. Also, some energy sources such as solar energy are good alternatives, but the cost will not be affordable to the poor women, especially in the third world. Lastly, a society should consider the appropriateness of technology when discussing the issue of alternate renewable energy. An energy source based on a technology that cannot be understood by the users will create more problems than the one it is supposed to solve.

CHAPTER SIX

The Sociocultural effects of Environmental Degradation on Communities

Introduction

The process whereby man adapts to his environment is called work.

Environments are defined as physical, cultural, and political. For humans to adapt and survive in their environments, they need to extract and transform the products that they obtain from nature to a form that will be socially convenient for their use.

Environmental degradation refers to a situation whereby the original natural quality of the environment becomes poorer because of increased usage—or rather, misusage—of nature. This may be a result of nonrechargeable resources that man's activities have depleted. It may be because external properties were allowed to mix with natural resources unchecked (a situation always referred to as pollution), or it may be a function of the usage rate going above the regeneration rate.

All these are apt to have serious negative consequences, which may be social, physical, and even environmental. This paper is, however, concerned only with the social effects of environmental degradation. It is our intention to examine its effects on man, his work, his living condition, and his leisure in Nigerian communities. Empirical evidence will be gathered to buttress our central focus which states that "there is an urgent need to curb environmental degradation in Nigeria because it is rapidly becoming life-threatening." Activities like pollution, bush burning, wildlife hunting, and vegetation depletion are specifically considered.

Environmental Degradation

Environmental degradation is a function of man. This agrees very well with the Marxian assertion that man is the maker of history. Whatever happens to the environment is made to happen by man, and incidentally, the consequences are always on man. Hence, they are called social consequences. The environment to be considered in this chapter includes

Land. This includes the physical land itself and minerals, including fossil fuel.
Water. Here we consider water for irrigation, for domestic use, and all water resources, including fishes and its entire species. We will also consider all kinds of pollution.

Atmosphere. We will consider all kinds of air pollution.
Vegetation and wildlife. We will consider repeated cultivation,
    bush burning, and desertification.
Human habitation. Here we consider urbanism, rural-urban
    migration, and all the vices surrounding it.

We refer to degradation in all these aspects. Because
of persistent human activity, their natural qualities are
reduced to the extent that their potential to support man's
adaptation to the environment becomes reduced. We
shall now examine evidence of degradation in all these
dimensions and their social consequences.

Land

Land has one of the most fundamental evidences of
degradation. This is not surprising, because the first work
known to man is the mixture of his own brute force to
extract things from land for his use. This has been referred
to differently in ages. It is called horticulture, agriculture,
pastoration, and the like. This extraction continues today
with more intensity and goes into other dimensions,
resulting into excessive land degradation. Today, man is
not only extracting through agriculture; he now mines. He
extracts fossil fuel solid mineral. The result of all these is a
huge rate of land degradation resulting into physical and
social consequences.

Land degradation has been life-threatening because
it results into shortage of food. This fact was first noticed
by Walter Rodney (1977), who wrote *How Europe*

Underdeveloped Africa. He gave an account of how the whites, because of their ignorance of African weather conditions, overcultivated the top African soil to the extent that they were left facing the problems of erosion. This made the yield of the soil become lower, which heralded the food crisis—a major consequence of which is environmental degradation today. It was also a major cause of rural-urban migration, which caused the problem for our cities.

Land degradation today is a reality. Evidence can be gathered from the following facts. Owing to colonial degradation of land, farmers today have resorted to using herbicides, fertilizers, pesticides, and other numerous chemicals that are doing damage to the land than helping. Land in the villages is becoming so arid and unproductive. This eventually leads the population to migrate to the cities, with the tales of woe following this huge movement of the human population to the cities. The village is devastated, no effective labor force is left there to work, and this results in low productivity of food and high prices in the cities. It also leads to all the vices in our cities, overusage of urban facilities, and crime resulting from unemployment and underemployment of the army of the largely unskilled laborers coming from these rural areas.

Pastoralists

Another evidence of degradation is the activities of the pastoralists in overgrazing and grazing in the farmlands. They even encourage bush burning so that grasses may grow quickly at the onset of rains in the areas they have burnt. In Northern Nigeria, the pastoralists sometimes get out of their routes to damage the farms of the farmers. These activities have resulted in grave social consequences. Its physical consequence is deforestation, desertification, and soil erosion. While socially it leads to hunger and interhuman or intergroup conflicts between these herdsmen and farmers, in most cases, these conflicts become so bloody that a whole village is wiped off the surface of the earth. This brings their attendant social problems of orphaning, poverty, hunger, and penury.

According to NEST (1991), pastoralists and nomads constitute one of the greatest problems to environmental degradation. Their movement with their cattle is supposed to have been initiated by nonavailability of forage and water for drinking (NEST 1991, 28) Nigeria has two seasons: the wet or rainy and the dry season. Grasses and pasture start growing at the onset of a new raining season. This gives a signal to the farmers to start planting, but at the same time, it becomes a signal to the pastoralists to start grazing. This double signal to two parties whose interests center on the same thing has resulted into untold conflicts between farmers and herdsmen. The farmer overgrazes areas to the extent that it results in devastation of the areas resulting into serious soil erosion. Soil erosion accounts for a large number of young men leaving their rural areas to cities, especially in the eastern parts of Nigeria where the land-to-man ratio is too small and the little land has been opened to serious erosion. Erosion is, year by year, eating up large proportions of the total land available for cultivation.

Land erosion by wind and rain is also being encouraged by animals (cattle), which trample the soil in large numbers, especially in the northern part of Nigeria. This renders most areas sterile, and aggravates the conflict between herdsmen and farmers. Empirical examples abound on this, especially in Northern Nigeria where cattle-rearing is one of the economic activities. The *National Concord* of December 1, 1989, reported a violent clash between Hausa farmers and Fulani cattle-rearers that claimed nine lives. This problem was said to be the result of an alleged destruction of a farm owned by Hausa by the Fulani cattle-rearers on November 16, 1989. The offensive was conducted like a full-scale war, and the whole Fulani settlement was sacked. This row left behind a very bad social consequence—orphans, widows, and widowers. Able-bodied men who were still in their productive years were killed. This will eventually affect food production. Such an incident is not isolated, but they occur frequently in the northern part of the country. In the same month in 1989, two persons were beheaded while three policemen were assaulted after a bloody communal clash between the Mumuye and the Fulani herdsmen of Sukani in the Jalingo area of the now Taraba State. This was as a result of the devastation of farmlands by the Fulani herdsmen (NEST 1991, 27). This problem is not only limited to the northern part of the country alone. It has been reported in Ibadan in the west, in Enugu in the east, and in the communities of the Middle Belt in Benue State. The *Daily Times* of April 21, 1981, reported that antiriot policemen had to wade into a ding-song "battle" between the Fulani herdsmen and some villagers in Mbayegh and Konshisha local government area of Benue State. The whole local government was almost deserted, and the economic and social activities, paralyzed.

This fact is well-known today and fraction efforts are being made to resolve this problem arising from environmental degradation of land by the pastoralists. The problem did not really stop and it continues to grow. It has engulfed the whole of Nigeria to the extent that it is being considered as serious as the Boko Haram insurgency or the Niger Delta Militants. It was serious during the Jonathan administration and it has risen to an alarming stage during Buhari anti-corruption regime. The sad point is that in 2015 and 2016 Nigerian have infused ethnic meaning into what started as an environmental problem.

Another serious social consequence is the health problems. Cattle is known to distribute disease to water and plants as they move along their routes. This is more so as it is sure that herdsmen do not secure the services of veterinary doctors. Hookworms, roundworms, and mites causing rabies are common diseases transferred to man. This causes a grave social consequence as the health bill of Nigeria increases through this environment neglect.

Water and Atmosphere (Air)

This is the environment that sustains man and other living things in the universe. Without water and oxygen, no life—including that of plants—can survive.

Water is a very useful gift of nature. It is useful for the normal functioning of the body, and it is also of immense use externally for each function as irrigation, laundry, personal hygiene, transport, and the like. In the same vein, without clean air, man will die in minutes, and environment health suffers in the face of a poor air situation in any given community.

Consequently, any negative effect on this important gift of nature will adversely affect man by creating serious negative social consequences.

A state of environmental degradation affecting water and air is called pollution. NEST (1991) defines water pollution as a situation whereby a water body is loaded with waste materials or heat such that its natural ability for self-purification can no longer cope with the situation. The quality of water deteriorates as undesirable changes take place in its physical, chemical, and biological properties. These changes may be sufficient to render the water unusable or inconvenient for domestic, recreational, and other uses (NEST 1991, 75–76).

Man has been the chief agent of water pollution. He pollutes the surface water by dumping lots of wastes, including human feces,. Most industries used to dump their wastes into fresh surface rivers. Evidence has shown that even the underground water is now being polluted by increasing use of fertilizers and other chemicals. Our industries dump their wastes, which sometimes contains DDT and other chemicals toxic to man into our lagoon and rivers. The rivers that drain our urban areas are totally filled up with wastes that need to be decomposed.

Social Consequences

Water pollution's social consequences are very bad and uncomfortable for man. Its effect can be considered in these dimensions: health-related and adaptation-related.

Water pollution prevents man from properly adapting to his environment by terminating the lives of aquatic animals that man uses as food. It sometimes also creates dangers to mans' health when he eats the aquatic animals that have been affected by the toxic chemicals dumped into these rivers. Scientists have submitted that organic wastes dumped into our rivers need to be decomposed by microorganisms referred to as decomposers. To do their work, these microorganisms need the same oxygen being used by the aquatic organisms to survive and perform their work. Eventually, they start competing with fishes and other forms of life in waters. The biological oxygen demand (BOD) of these microorganisms increases directly with the volume of the pollutants. Consequently aquatic animals die in the lagoons and rivers where large amount of pollutants are present. Such rivers, apart from hurting humans by rendering him a hungry man, also contribute to his ill health. Viruses and bacteria harmful to man grow in such rivers.

This eventually results in epidemics of cholera, typhoid fever, and river blindness, which are common ailments today. In most urban areas the onset of the rainy season is a big headache. This is because the dry human feces are flushed into rivers and their viruses of typhoid fever, cholera, and the like are reactivated. The effect of this, especially if the water is used for domestic consumption and feeding, is the outbreak of cholera, dysentery, and other kinds of disease. A very common disease caused by mere touching of the polluted water is bilharzia. The prevalence of the incidence of guinea worm in most states of Nigeria-Kwara, Ondo, and Benue State point to the fact of a high incidence of water pollution. The result of this is high health bills for both the people and the governments. Life expectancy is short, and the happiness of man in this situation is not guaranteed.

Atmosphere/Air

This environment has been highly polluted in the universe as well as Nigeria. This environment has been mostly polluted by inefficient and wasteful fossil fuel use. This has been aggravated by incessant bush burning by nomads and the like. The unabated high rate of fuelwood felling and gas flaring in our refineries contribute to the air and atmosphere pollution in Nigeria. NEST (1990) identifies some major causes of air pollution, among which are wastes disposed by burning, road traffic and other forces that raise dust on the roads, natural causes like pollens and the like.

Consequences

The social consequence of air pollution is mostly on health. Most of the lung disease problems being experienced in the developing nation today are functions of air pollution. Researches show that those people working in factories where they breathe in solid and carbon dioxide waste have a higher probability of suffering from lung disease than those not exposed to such hazards.

A very alarming fact coming from air pollution is its effect on the climate and the survival of the future generation. Experts have agreed that fossil fuel is not only unreliable in term of renewable characteristics, but their effects are also detrimental to the future survival of this planet because of their role in environmental degradation by causing atmospheric pollution.

We are therefore examining the effect of the use of fossil fuel energy on the accumulation of greenhouse gases like CO_2 and SO_2 (carbon dioxide and sulphur dioxide). It has been established that fossil fuel has a direct effect on their accumulation. These effects will eventually result in a 3°C increase in world temperature in the year 2090.

It was noted that climate changes occur because of increase concentration of atmospheric carbon dioxide (CO_2). The preindustrial concentration of CO_2 was only 280 per million parts of air, by volume (ppm). The ppm increased to 340 in 1980 and might rise to 560 before the year 2050.

The effect of this on environment is a disruption of agricultural and forestry ecosystems and flooding of lowland coastal areas. It will also disturb marine fisheries and food chains. This will have a socioeconomic effect, as agricultural trade will collapse. Eventually this will affect the health of people as food intake will drop. This is of tremendous effect to women. At the time of pregnancy, women need a lot of food to have a healthy fetus. One the food chain is broken, women are in danger. This will also affect them as the homemakers. Once there are climatic changes affecting the food, the home—which is a cherished prize of women—becomes the victim. In addition, the situation affects the depletion of the ozone layer. In fact, deadly diseases that are developing today, such as AIDS and ebola virus and mad cow disease, might be traced to the degradation of the environment by the unrestricted use of present energy sources—fossil fuel.

Vegetation and Rural and Urban Life

Man has polluted his habitats, rural or urban. He has depleted the vegetation and has killed to extinction some useful wildlife in the forests.

Experts asserted that the volumes of solid waste that will be generated for environmental degradation in Nigerian cities will rise to over fifteen million tons by the year 2009 (NEST 1991, 240). There is no open space for recreation in these cities as houses are built so close because of the economic importance of the urban land. In cities like Maiduguri, there are little or no ventilation in the houses, and buildings utilize common walls. This causes serious ventilation problems. There is no consistent system of waste disposal in most urban areas while the rural dwellers have no toilets and the like. People even defecate wherever they like, even in streams where they will eventually drink.

Desertification and erosion with their great social consequences result from mans' attitude to wildlife degradation because their natural habitats were being invaded by man.

The yearly bush burning affects the preservation of our wildlife. This has affected man because we have not allowed commensalism to flourish. The gains of man may be lost from animals, but man will lose on both sides when there are no animals—the loss of which will be beneficial to man.

Nigerian vegetation is becoming extinct. It seems there is no vegetation untouched by men in this country. The pressure on Nigerian vegetation is like the pressure on urban social services. They are both caused by an increase in pollution. However, the degradation in vegetation is a function of neglect of modern agricultural technology.

Farmers have to resort into always shifting cultivation and cultivating virgin forests in order to survive. If technology is appropriate, it would have been possible to have forest reservations because a high yield will be achieved on very little portions of land.

The effect of all this environmental degradation is very devastating to man. The loss of vegetation eventually causes loss of wildlife and man loses the source of protein from that source. Too much grazing and cultivation led to desertification and loss of food.

All these are social consequences of environmental degradation. The effect of all these result into the large rural-urban movement which is causing problems in our cities today.

Conclusion

This chapter has discussed the social consequences of environmental degradation. It became clear from our analysis that if this is unchecked, life on this planet generally and in this country in particular will be unbearable. It has encouraged the large influx of people into the cities, which in turn, has generated vice, poverty, penury, and crimes. It has affected the health of the population in both the urban and rural areas. It is even threatening life on this planet by the depletion of the ozone layer. This is seen to be cause of all the new diseases such as the AIDS virus, ebola, and mad cow disease. It has depleted our wildlife and is now contributing to desertification. It is very necessary that a check is put on this environmental degradation so that life in this country will become bearable again.

CHAPTER SEVEN

Tension Centers: Human Rights Violations and the Elites' Victim-Blaming Attitudes

Introduction

The effect of the government and Nigerian elites' mechanism of tension management is examined utilizing historical and contemporary observations. It was established that the government and the power elites in Nigeria defined those individual and groups who have knowledge of the authorities' method of economic exploitation as tension centers and troublemakers who should be controlled. Consequently, measures referred to as mechanisms of tension management are embarked upon by the enactment of harsh laws and policies that affect Nigerian human rights negatively. Evidence was produced from the colonial administration and contemporary Nigerian government's policies. The paper concludes that a nondirective, people-centered (rather than government-directed), and externally imposed mechanism of tension management will bring necessary peace to Nigeria.

Keywords: mechanism of tension management, tension center, nondirective approach, historical process, human right

Introduction: Tension Management

This chapter examines the various mechanisms of tension management in Nigeria in order to determine how they affect human rights. Our basic aim is to identify the effect of tension management mechanisms on human rights conditions in order to proffer possible solutions for policy implications and implementations.

Tension in the context of this chapter is interactional, and it can be defined as a situation whereby two actors have reasons not to trust themselves, resulting in an inherent conflict based on hatred and fear of each other. Tension can be analyzed, utilizing the Marxian *historical process,* as a creation of man, and it is dependent on the interaction between men. Any kind of interaction that creates a strain in a relationship between two actors can result in tension. In actual fact, tension follows a situation in which the interests of two interactants are involved, and each of the parties believes that the other member constitutes a hindrance to his or her progress. That is why tension consists of the elements of fear and conflict, which make tension also become an independent variable. Fear and conflict cannot be tolerated long by humans, and the interactants always attempt to develop mechanisms for the management of the tension that generated them.

The two contending parties are not always equally matched in their ability and capability to introduce the mechanism that could resolve the conflict and fear generated by the tension. The stronger, in most cases, dictates the terms and conditions for the introduction of the mechanism for the management of tension, which is mostly imposed on the weaker. The rights of the weaker are not always protected or taken into consideration. This is always regarded as an externally imposed mechanism of tension management by the weaker on which the mechanism is imposed. This externally imposed mechanism is of most interest in the examination of human rights processes in Nigeria, because most tension management mechanisms are dictated by the superior, the governments, and the powerful elites to control the poor masses without any consultation with them. In fact, such a mechanism was well explained in Karl Marx's theory of ideology where he argued that the powerful elite in society only enact laws that will help further their interests and protect their capital. The second type of tension-management mechanism is people-centered. This represents a rule of conduct that has been arrived at by the people out of practice. In many cases, it becomes part of the people's culture, and it is manifested in the customs of the people and may sometimes develop into laws or conventions whose authority may be more than that of law.

Tension Center

A tension center is defined within the context of this chapter as the particular event or people that an actor believes have the potential of producing an effect that will be disastrous to his (actor's) aspiration, intention, or program. Such a center, the particular actor believes, should be controlled so that the anticipated negative tension to be generated by the action of the center will not materialize. The actor regards the "alter" (actors at the identified center) as antagonistic and dysfunctional to his aspirations. The control strategy, otherwise referred to as the mechanism of tension management, is always initiated by the superior actor who, invariably, expects to gain if the tension is controlled. However the alter (the identified opposition) will not always agree with such mechanisms, especially, if it affects his fundamental human rights. In most cases, tension-management mechanisms always affect the rights of the weaker because the aim of the initiator is to protect him (initiator) against others. The degree to which this happens is a function of the actors' (initiator) objective, class, and ethnic group.

A review of the past tension-management efforts in Nigeria shows that different tension centers have been identified by the government, employers of labor, ethnic group leaders, and political or power elites. These various actors defined the workers, defenseless market women, urban poor, labor unions, and university students and academia as the tension centers. These powerful actors eventually initiated tension-management mechanisms to manage the tensions created by the centers that, in most cases, disregarded the human rights of the citizens. Students and defenseless women were killed without any compensation as a rule to contain protests. Citizens were imprisoned without trial to protect official secrets, and employees were sacked and retrenched without any due process.

Tension Center Identification

The Nigerian governments (federal and state) are the major employers of labor, and they control almost all economic activities in the country. The political leaders and government officials loot the treasury and mismanage public funds. Awareness of this always draws the ire of university students, market women, underpaid workers, and the masses who always protest to demand justice. These categories of Nigerians have therefore been identified as tension centers by the governments. To manage the tension centers, successive governments, civilian and military, have enacted laws and promulgated decrees as tension-management mechanisms that negatively impacted peoples' human rights. Punitive laws and regulations aimed at protecting public officials have been promulgated just to check the excesses of the identified tension centers. The question that will be addressed here is "how successful are the mechanisms they have propounded?" Can laws and decrees alone succeed in managing and controlling tensions in Nigeria?

Similarly, the employers of labor, especially at the private sector of the economy, regard their employees and the labor organizations as the centers of tension. Employers (both public and private sectors) have therefore succeeded in lobbying the government to institute laws and regulations to prevent workers from demanding for improved welfare and working conditions.

Elite ethnic group leaders define members of opposing ethnic groups as the tension centers and compete for juicy government positions. This action mostly creates interethnic conflict as ordinary ethnic group members always fight to support their ethnic group leaders. Laws were enacted to manage interethnic tension through the utilization of national character and quotas rather than a merit-based system to distribute national positions and benefits. The question that should still be considered is whether these mechanisms have actually produced the intended tension management and interethnic unity?

Tension Management: The Colonial Experience

The starting point for the practice of mechanisms of tension management in Nigeria should be traced to the colonial period. The colonial administration identified its own tension center in relation to the British administration's goal of using Nigeria's vast agricultural and mineral resources for the development of British industries. The British defined the educated Nigerians who were agitating for freedom from British foreign oppression as the tension center that should be destroyed. Early Nigerian educated individuals such as Herbert Macaulay, Dr. Azikiwe, Mbonu Ojike, and Awolowo resented the slavery condition imposed on Nigerians by the British administration. Nkrumah lamented a situation he described as the selfishness of the British administration, whereby they failed to establish a single processing industry for any of the raw materials extracted from the African colonies. Africa was likened to the "drawers of waters and hewers of wood" for the British. Walter Rodney analyzed this fact in his account of how Europe underdeveloped Africa when he observed that the closer an African country was to a European colonial master, the poorer that nation became. He therefore shows that there is a direct relationship between African national poverty and association with Europe. The early educated Nigerians disagreed with Lord Lugard's explanation of the dual mandate of civilizing and evangelizing the Nigerians as the official goals of British imperialism. They believe that the inherent goals of the British were exploitation and decapitalization of Nigeria to benefit Britain. The British identified the educated natives as the tension center, and engaged in numerous tension-management mechanisms, which impacted negatively on their human rights, to control the situation. Educated natives became fugitive offenders in their own land and were prevented from doing any work that would involve instructing the young ones in schools so that the Nigerian youths might not be brainwashed. Nnamdi Azikiwe, after obtaining a double master's degree from Lincoln University in the USA was considered too dangerous to teach in a Nigerian school. The British created a division between the traditional elite (emirs, *obi*s, and *oba*s) who were the rulers before the advent of the British colonial administration, and the educated elite through the system of indirect rule.

Indirect rule ensured the total control of Nigerian people by allowing the traditional rulers to act *as if* they were the real rulers. The British used them as the mask to plunder Nigerian society and cart away the natural resources. The traditional rulers, acting on the advice and instruction of the British, meted heavy punishment on any recalcitrant youth that dared went against the British administration. Awolowo (1948) declared that indirect rule was the system whereby the British collaborated with the existing oppressors (traditional rulers) to further oppress the already oppressed (Nigerian masses). They took away the power from its traditional base by pretending that they were enhancing the traditional rulers' power but eventually turned the traditional rulers to mere tools used to mete out punishment to the educated agitators for self-government. The losers in this British colonial adventure were the Nigerian people who were unaware that the oppressors had changed. The traditional rulers, on the other hand, were unaware that instead of having an enhanced status, they had become the masks worn by British administrators to rule the people. The British, however, became alarmed when a crop of educated natives started campaigning to make the people become aware of their political environment. They formed interest groups and political organizations— prominent among these were the West African Students Union (WASU), the Nigerian National Democratic Party (NNDP), and the National Convention of Nigerians and Cameroons (NCNC). The colonial government reacted swiftly to all these and declared them as tension centers. Draconian laws and policies were enacted to tame these "recalcitrant" groups and their related collaborators such as the associations of market women and labor. Nnoli believes that it was this colonial style of government and system of tension management mechanism that gave birth to Nigerian ethnicity. The tension-management mechanism of the British administration played ethnic groups against themselves by favoring some ethnic groups against others. Elements from one group were denied access to the resources of the nation while others were allowed to benefit. It was a deliberate action on the part of the British administration that the Western type of education was not introduced in Northern Nigeria so that the traditional rulers would always support them (Oshuntokun). This resulted in a Nigeria where the South possessed an army of Western-educated people and the North does not. The discrepancy in numbers and quality of educated population between the South and the North today is one of the causes of mistrust between the two regions and the major cause of interethnic conflict. The British also handled any case of protest against any action of the colonial government with heavy hand without any consideration for the protesters' human rights. This fact could be detected in the way the Enugu coal mine workers' demonstration was treated, which resulted in the Enugu bloodbath of 1949 and the Aba women's riots. Hundreds of miners and unarmed women fell to the bullets of the British administrators' soldiers for daring to request for justice and human rights enforcement. Most of the policies of the British were made to manage tensions that would result in their perpetuation of power and the discrediting of the educated natives. The British colonial administration encouraged ethnicity; entrenched the rule of the feudal *oba*s, *obi*s, and emirs;

and repressed laborers, poor workers, farmers, and above all, women in their bid to practice their own version of mechanisms of tension management. It can be detected from the above that the colonial practice did not respect the fundamental human rights of the people. The British colonialists thought tension was deemed to have been well managed once the interests of the British government were protected. That was why they created inequity and inequality in all spheres of societal activities.

Postcolonial and Present

The defined centers of tension and, consequently, the identified victims of mechanisms of tension management are not significantly different in postcolonial Nigeria today. The actors who define tension centers are no longer the foreigners; they are the new Nigerian elites—some of whom were formerly defined as tension centers in the colonial period—and their offspring who have become political elites. The new Nigerian elites define any group or individuals who are opposed to their insatiable desire for material accumulation through the looting of public funds as tension centers and the enemies of the society. The new elite saw the urban and rural poor, the market women, labor unions, students, academia, and farmers as tension centers. According to Nnoli (1978), their major goal "is to maintain social, political, economic and religions domination of the people." In order to achieve this, the new elite created mechanisms of tension management, which are non–people friendly to protect themselves from attack. Having identified the Nigerian people as the tension center, their next action was to identify what they should do to manage the tension being created. However, the mechanisms of tension management they created are instruments for the maintenance of their domination on the people.

One of the tensions emphasized by the power elite is interethnic tension. Several authors (Nnoli, 1978, Ogunnika 1994) agree that the interethnic problem was created by the nature of the mechanisms of interethnic tension management created by the new Nigerian elites and the political leaders to manage ethnic tensions. In order to solve the problem, the power elite employed two tension-management techniques, which are (1) the quota system, and (2) the federal character. The two systems are supposed to prevent the domination by any ethnic group over the others. National positions, such as appointments to boards of parastatals, ministerial positions, and the like will be distributed equally among the states, taking into consideration the factors of ethnicity and religion. It is a system that the political leaders believed would ensure equality for all Nigerians irrespective of states of origin, religion, or ethnic orientation. However, our observation of the workings of this system shows that it is a diversionary technique aimed at preoccupying the attention of the people to prevent them from realizing the damage the power elite are inflicting on the society.

- It does not respect the fundamental human rights of the people.
- It is discriminatory in approach.

- It is being manipulated to the advantage of the elites so that the underdogs will always be disunited.

The power elite in Nigeria will hold on to power as long as the Nigerian ethnic groups are disunited. Quota system as a mechanism of tension management made interethnic unity impossible, because Nigerians under the quota system and national character are only assured of a share in the national cake through their respective ethnic, state, and religion affiliations. The practice makes the Nigerians conscious of their ethnic and religious affiliations before identifying themselves as Nigerians. Since rewards in society and social outcomes are predicated on one's ethnic and religious groups, ethnic rivalry becomes more intense, and interethnic jealousy and rivalry abounds in all aspects of Nigerian society.

The elites and political leaders intentionally reward one ethnic group less than another to create problems. The formula utilized to distribute income into the consolidated account due to the thirty-six Nigerian states favor some states more than the other. This gave rise to ethnic militant groups such as Agbekoya in the former Western Region. In recent times, it led to the emergence of the Movement for the Emancipation of Niger Delta (MEND), which paralyzed the whole economic activity in the Southeastern Nigeria. It was this system that was mostly responsible for the insurgence of Boko Haram a radical Islamic movement, which has been responsible for the killings of thousands of Nigerians and a spate of bombings in churches and public buildings in Northern Nigeria. The political elites derive their legitimacy by proclaiming to be the champions of their ethnic and religious groups and publicly advocating more for their groups under the quota system and national character. The elites therefore become relevant in national politics as champions of local (ethnic or religious) courses, and they become more successful when there are intense interethnic tensions.

Evidence of corrupt practices and the large amount of money found in the accounts of corrupt government officials shows that the elites were just pretending to be ethnic group champions so that they might enrich themselves. In addition, the institutional approach meant to curtail the actions of corrupt political officeholders was not performing its duties. Most of the corrupt officials arraigned before the courts and the special anticorruption tribunals were never convicted. It was on record that the only big-time Nigerian politician ever convicted, James Ibori, the former governor of Delta state, was jailed in London after the Nigerian tribunal and courts had cleared him of corruption.

One is alarmed at the huge sum converted to their personal use by the new Nigerian elites, and one wonders how their claims to be ethnic champions has ensured the tolerance of society to the economic crimes they commit. Numerous examples could also be cited during the probes of second-republic politicians and the Nigerian military-politicians who looted without any fear.

State creation in Nigeria is a clever interethnic tension-management mechanism used to perfect the system of public-fund stealing in Nigeria. Rationalized as an attempt to alleviate the fears of the minority, the power elite created more states in Nigeria, but in actual fact, ethnic political leaders wanted the new states as empires for themselves where they can steal more of the public fund. Opinions reasoned that the rights of most people in the new states were not taken into consideration as a majority of them fared better in the former states. Families were moved, jobs were lost, and children were disrupted from their normal school environments, this situation supports the opinion that the creation of states cannot manage tension but could create more. The creation of states also aggravates the process of what Cohen (1969) referred to as detribalization. This is a situation in which rather than the people of different ethnicities forgetting their differences, the creation of the state acts as a motivator for aggravating the feeling of differences.

Conclusions and Recommendations

We have attempted an analysis of the government and powerful elites' sponsored mechanism of tension management in Nigeria. Our analysis shows that such mechanisms are not achieving their objectives. This observation is based on the fact that the mechanisms are instruments of the power elites to further entrench their dominant and exploitative position on the masses. The resistance that always comes from the masses turns these tension-management mechanisms to tension-generated mechanisms. One reason for this is based on the elites' approach and method of execution of tension-management mechanism. The elite based mechanism of tension management in Nigeria utilizes what the experts call the directive approach to the solution of people's problems.

This approach sees the people as stupid and nonintelligent and that their problems can only be solved by intelligent power elite. Consequently, the government, in collaboration with the powerful elites, enacts laws that will help the elite to oppress the masses in order to force tension created by the elite's greed for material and power as mechanism for tension management. The people, however, always rationalize the situation and understand the true intention of the mechanisms; hence, instead of managing tension, the mechanisms create more tensions. The elite's tension-management policies and laws, being directive, are full of contradictions that the people always reject, an action which always causes new tensions. In view of the above, we therefore recommend that a proper tension-management mechanism should be people-centered, and the methodology to be utilized should follow what T. R. Batten refers to as the nondirective approach. The nondirective approach believes that the people whose tension is to be managed should be the ones to decide the mechanisms of the tension management. If this is done, it will create some advantages:

1. *Voluntary obedience.* Being contributors to the genesis of tension-management mechanisms' policy, the people will be motivated to obey them.
2. *Devoid of class domination.* It will not be possible for some groups or classes to use the mechanisms as instruments of domination.
3. *Lasting peace and harmony among ethnic groups.* Such a system will bring a lasting peace to Nigeria, and it will ensure respect for the peoples' fundamental human rights.

The last question is not what should be done, but how can it be done. Our response to this is that researchers have been investigating people-centered mechanisms of tension management in Nigeria. In one of such researches, Ogunnika (1994) discovered that we need not enact any laws in parliament nor promulgate decrees but create a favorable environment for the persistence of what he calls the "people-centered mechanism of tension management." This is because the result of his research shows that over the years, ordinary people in their everyday lives have discovered rules governing their conduct in their various daily activities. Such rules make interaction possible and prevent tension, and the rules are not in law books, but they have become part of the daily lives and activities of the people. The people utilize them in different situations: in their relation with themselves, in the markets where market groups and market languages are created, in work places, in schools, in politics, and in leisure. In fact, Ogunnika asserts that it is the use of these tension-management mechanisms that have been preventing the outbreak of conflict that is being generated by the power elites' version of tension-management mechanisms. It is our hope that Nigerians will begin to live better lives and their fundamental human rights will become guaranteed when the mechanisms for tension management becomes more people-centered rather than being dictated by the power elite.

CHAPTER EIGHT

Contemporary Black Migrants in American Society

Introduction

This chapter discusses the conditions of the immigrants from black African countries in American societies. This class of immigrants has the physical characteristics of the African American but is different culturally in terms of language, family life, and other sociocultural dimensions. These characteristics affect his perception of himself and how he is perceived in the society and, in large extent, affect how he is treated in society in terms of access to resources and social amenities.

The chapter utilizes the interpretative methodology to arrive at the different perceptions of the black immigrant in the society. We thereafter advance the argument that the plight of the black African is a function of the meanings given to him from the various perceptions. His status in American society is therefore a function of the preceptor and the perception.

The chapter identifies different perceptions leading to various meanings of the black African immigrant in the United States. The perceptions discussed in the paper include the following:

(a) *Self-perception.* The configuration and the presentation of the self by the black African immigrant. This has affected the status of the black African immensely in recent times. It is believed that some black immigrants are soiling the good names of this class of immigrants by engaging in criminal activities and deceptions. A school of thought, however, rationalizes that the subjective meaning to this by the Africans is to appear very "smart," believing he can outmaneuver other society members. This school believes that this "innovative" character is a function of the hardship being suffered by the immigrants and therefore should be regarded as a coping mechanism. The crimes are therefore a kind of social insurance against discrimination and lower status positions accorded them in society, the theorist seems to believe.

(b) *Exogenous perceptions.* This is how the black African is being perceived by other elements of the larger American society. Our discussions are divided into two: how he is being perceived by African Americans and how he is being perceived by the other Americans, including the whites. In analyzing the perception of the others, we discussed the role of history and the common aspiration of the black immigrant and the African American. We were able to establish that education and social class affect the perception the African American has of the black immigrant. This eventually affects the relationship and cooperation between them. The others, including the white's population, are perceived by the African immigrant based on the presentation of the self. Their (the whites and others) perceptions change as the African American's self-presentation changes. This eventually affects the social status accorded him in the society today. The status of the African immigrant was very high in the early twentieth century, when scholars such as Azikiwe and Nkrumah came to study in the USA, but the status has reduced today based on their poor presentation of self.

The paper concludes by discussing how the various perspectives could be regarded as the determinant of the position of the black African immigrant in contemporary American society. We therefore agree with Stanford Lyman that the sociology of black African immigrants in America is yet to begin.

Immigration Prior to 1800

It has been established that the African presence in the new world predates Columbus's adventure to Africa (Nwachuku and Zigwe, 2006). But the first real immigration to America by the black Africans was the forced migration referred to as slavery. This happened between 1619 and 1807, first to Virginia and later spreading all over the new world. Their descendants today are known as African Americans. This paper is not so much concerned about this group. We are concerned about the black population who came after the abolition of the trade and during the height of the civil right movement up till today. Our focus on this group is to describe their coping mechanisms in terms of family life, work, leisure, religion, and the like and their interactions with their hosts of all races.

The Early African Voluntary Migration

Authorities on this subject (immigration) submit that African immigrants constitute the smallest percentage of the total immigrants' population in the United States. According to John Arthur (2000), this group comes to United States principally from Nigeria, South Africa, Liberia, Ghana, and Kenya. Voluntary migration to the United States from Africa was initially very small after the abolition of slave trade. Between 1808 and 1900, only 350 immigrants came to the United States shores from black Africa (Arthur 2000). Gordon (1988), however, submits that this figure increased tremendously to over 31,000 during the colonial rules in Africa. Despite the increase since the end of colonial rule, immigrants from black Africa constitute only about 1% of the total immigrants in the United States. In 1910, Peter Roberts believes that the African (black) immigrant in America did not constitute enough blocks of immigrants to be studied. He omitted them in his book ***Immigrant Races in North America***. In his own words,

> *In the classified list, forty-five people are mentioned. Of these the African (blacks), the Cuban are not treated in the present work. (This is because) The African immigrants are lost in Negro population and are seldom thought of as forming people.*

However, eighty years later in 1993, the African immigrant population is thought of as very important to the extent that a Ford Foundation grant was awarded to study them (Oluponna 1993). The whole population of Africans (blacks) entering the United States in 1900 was only 33,000. But today, this group numbers more than a million (Oluponna 1993).

Theoretical Orientation

Theorists were excited over race relations, especially in America as the new world. Lyman especially concluded that it was in the field of race relations that the theorist tried to display sociological imagination most. Despite all these, Lyman lamented that the theorist has not done enough to explain social relationships among African Americans. He therefore suggested that the sociology of African American is yet to begin. He did not agree with the explanation of both the positivists and the Marxists on the sociology of black Americans.

Theoretical consideration of the plight of African American can be attempted through two contending theories or major schools: nomothetic and idiographic in sociology. Interpretative theories believe that analysis of their plight in American society can be done by the actors—the African immigrants themselves. It believes that going otherwise will provide observer's fallacy. However, positivist theorists say that it can be analyzed scientifically from the standpoint of reason and observation. It is believed that an order of natural setting can be discovered of the relationship, and the causative factors of why things happen the way they happen can be discovered. The positivists will not agree with the notion that most of the behaviors of the African American and African immigrants are reactions to societal conditions created by powers too strong for them to control. Instead it is believed that what is being observed is not caused by anybody but a result of a natural predetermined force that will happen as it has been set. They believe that society has an inherent mechanism of self-regulation that cannot be wished away.

The Marxists from the idiographic school, however, believes that, the plight of African immigrants and blacks is a result of inequalities and inequity, which results in availability of less opportunity for blacks and African immigrants. The negative conditions found among this group cannot be blamed on them. They (Marxists) believe that man is the maker of his destiny, but he does not create under his own volition. He is forced to do it by some uncontrollable powers over him. The actions of the African immigrant right from his decision to leave his country, to what he does and how he does it in America are dictated to him by powers beyond his control. He cannot control the politicians who plundered the economy and looted the treasury which made life unbearable for him, as in the case of Nigeria. In America, he has no power over the system of meaning societies, groups, and races (including the African Americans) gave to the African immigrants, which resulted in the race relations that affected him adversely. Both schools of thought explain some variances in the analyses of the African immigrant in America, but it seems that more variances were explained by the Marxists.

Characteristics of African Immigrants

The immigrants from black African countries are mostly the cream of the societies they came from. Most of them are highly educated and the best and brightest in their fields. They were forced out of their countries because of the deplorable conditions of unemployment, underemployment, and harsh living conditions in their countries. Most of them were initially educated in the West (Britain and America). They have been well socialized into the freedom in Western democracy and were eager to demonstrate these in their countries. The culture and political climate there did not support this. Most, therefore, left their countries out of frustration for their inability to utilize the knowledge gained in the West for the good of their countries. A large number actually fled their countries. They have been marked as security risks by the governments and, if they tarry any longer, may vanish or face incarceration. Some are political refugees. A large number are youths who are still strong and are ambitious to obtain qualitative education and enjoy the "bright lights" dreams that they believe America is. They are therefore assets that can be harnessed to useful projects in American societies. On this, Nwachuku and Zizwe declare:

> Those that migrate are out are potential middle classes in their respective countries . . . They brought with them creative talents, especially, intellectual that have enhanced the contributions of black people to human civilizations.

However, the immigrants were underrated in their country of sojourn in America. The authors Nwachuku and Zizwe (2006) lamented that instead of harnessing them as resources

> The United States to which the Africans migrate feel burdened by their presence. Thus, during the first decade of 21st century, immigration became a major issue in the United States and other European nations. These countries pass stringent measures that would make immigration to them difficult.

The African migrants suffer a lot from name-calling and labeling. Despite the fact that he shows love to the African American through history up to the present time, the later seems not to trust him. Because of his high education, the legal residents among them secure good jobs. The African American sees this as a cheat on them. They, in many private conversations, usually say that the African immigrants resort to taking the African American quota of national cake after their forefathers sold the African American into slavery. This is in negation of the symbiotic relationship between them originally in fighting racism in America and colonialism in Africa.

The Early Twentieth Century: The Courageous Pioneers

Voluntary migration of Africans started after the abolition of slave trade in 1807. However, it seems Africans were reluctant to move to America, as only 350 immigrants showed between 1891 and 1900 (Arthur 2000). This, however, increased between 1900 and 1950, during the period of colonial rule in Africa, when over 30,000 immigrants came to United States (Gordon 1998). Our concern here is with this group of African immigrants who are labeled courageous pioneers here because of the following reasons:

a. They blazed the trail regardless of uncertainties surrounding how they would be treated in the USA, bearing in mind the recent abolition of the slave trade,

b. The conditions in the United States were becoming economically intolerable, even for the whites and the African Americans. It was therefore a credit that these early twentieth-century pioneers were able to come, stay, and achieve. They created a favorable perception for the African immigrant. They had their heads on their shoulders despite the harsh conditions of the time. Kevern Verney described the economic suffering of that time thus:

The Wall Street Crash and the Great Depression that followed had a profound impact on the lives of nearly all Americans . . . Economically insecure and with little in the way of saving, even during the comparative prosperity of the 1920s, most African Americans were ill equipped to meet the hardship of the 1930s. Racial discrimination added to the sufferings, with blacks typically being the last to be hired and the first fired.

c. The activities of the pre-1920 immigrants benefited the society, especially the blacks with whom they teamed up to conduct the civil rights campaign. They teamed up to set the pace of freedom from colonial rule for African countries. Such cooperation is seen in the relationship between Du Bois and Kwame Nkrumah of Ghana (a member of the 1920s migration). Du Bois eventually died in Ghana, Africa. These great feats by the early migrants were preformed under harsh situations. Despite this situation, they did not go into crime or other objectionable activities as found among immigrants today. This group created a good perception for the African immigrants. Verney (2000) described the harsh situation under which they operated:

By 1931, over 40 percent of African Americans in Pittsburg were homeless and unemployed, and the situation was similar in all in all other leading cities. In 1932, 30 percent of Blacks in Chicago were out of work, 37 percent in Detroit, 33 percent in Cleveland, 28 percent in Philadelphia, and 25 percent in New York City.

The early migrants were subjected to cultural shocks and the inhumanity of man to man, which described the numerous acts of lynching of the blacks in America in this period. It was recorded that fifty-seven blacks were lynched during the presidency of Herbert Hoover between 1928 and 1933, yet he refused to pass the antilynching law referred to as the Dyer Bill. He refused state intervention to help the victims of unemployment, as he believed this is contrary to the principle of market mechanism. The early 1920s, African migrants faced a lot of physical discomfort, as they mostly lived in cities where the blacks suffered physical and health problems. It was on record that up to 1940, 70 percent of black homes had neither electricity nor running water (Verney 2000). Most first-generation African leaders were products of this early migration. Among them were Kwame Nkrumah of Ghana, Nnamdi Azikiwe of Nigeria, and a host of others. They later utilized their American experience to improve social and economic conditions in their countries. Most importantly, they utilized their experience in civil rights agitation to obtain independence for their respective countries.

The early 1900s, migrants' actions created positive perceptions for the immigrants in America, as their objective was lofty. The society they lived in still perceived them as worthy and important up till today. Proof to this lies in many things created to remember them and the numerous honors bestowed on them during their lifetime by the institutions they were connected with. Nnamdi Azikiwe and Kwame Nkrumah were awarded the honorary degrees of doctor of humane letters by their universities. Azikiwe was allowed to be a professor at Lincoln University after his education. Lincoln University has named a prominent building in the university after Azikiwe and Nkrumah. These early immigrants also perceived themselves and their society of sojourn in a positive way. Paul Lee, describing Nkrumah's sojourn in America, declared that

> in the 20th century, probably no one except Marcus Garvey did more to bring freedom and dignity to the black people worldwide than Kwame Nkrumah . . . It was his American sojourn that shaped Nkrumah into leading the pan-Africanist of the later half of the 20th century.

Nnamdi Azikiwe of Nigeria saw the importance of higher education in Nation building in America. He nursed the idea of a Nigerian University in the early 1930s and approached prominent Nigerians to contribute toward the achievement of the noble goal. The university was, however, not established at that time, but he kept his vision in sight. It finally materialized as the University of Nigeria when he became the first president of Nigeria after Nigerian independence.

The early migrants were futuristic and integrated very well with the progressives in America. It was on record that they attended meetings with civil rights leaders and joined their associations. Nkrumah recounted in his autobiography, *Ghana*, "I acquainted myself with as many political organizations that I could." The groups he talked about included the National Urban League and the National Association for the Advancement of the Colored People (NAACP). Nkrumah met and became friendly with Du Bois who was called the father of pan-Africanism. American life was regarded as a training ground for the 1900s immigrant as demonstrated by Nkrumah. They showed this in their pursuit of scholarship, their choice of friends, and their stoical characteristic to everything.

Underlying Causes of Contemporary Migrations from Africa

Migration from black Africa to United States today has increased tremendously. This is due to the positive perception of American ways of life in these countries. Theoretically, one can explain the situation through the "bright light" theory of human migration. The youths in African countries are nowadays exposed to American life, which is accessible to them through new cybernetics and Internet technology. During the time of Nkrumah and Azikiwe, it took several months before immigrants could communicate with their parents and friends at home. Nowadays, it takes fractions of a second for cell phones, which are now available everywhere. An event that happens in USA today is watched as it happens in African countries. Through television news and Internet connections, youths have created a mental presence and union with America while in Africa. What they only need to add is their physical presence through migration. The youths in these countries believe in the superiority of American education today. This has been reinforced by the policy of their various governments, which adopted American type of education (Okafor 2003). During the colonial era, American education was looked down upon, but the social, economic, and technological development recorded by the USA since World War II convinced the third-world population of the superiority of the USA in the field of education, and they were eager to taste it.

This push factor is reinforced by the thought that America is a paradise where everything can be transformed to money. The youths in Nigeria were encouraged to migrate to USA after seeing Hakeem Olajuwon becoming a millionaire (in USA dollars) through basketball, which could have been nothing in Nigeria. The attitudes of immigrants on visits to African nations encourage migration, as they almost show that money is easy to get in the USA. They spent lavishly in parties, rode in cars that the topmost civil servant or even politician cannot buy. Their houses were palatial and furnished lavishly.

Many factors, ranging from economic, political, inequity and injustice, and natural disasters also push the African immigrants from their countries. After the exit of the first-generation leaders of Africa and even during their times, it became apparent that the high-scale corruption and mismanagement cannot help the economies of these states. Eventually, the economy collapsed, and the huge population haad no choice but to run away from home. There was high unemployment and a scarcity of necessities. These nations, such as Nigeria, had to create a commission to monitor the distribution of such commodities that are labeled essential. In the list are salt, rice, detergent, soap, sugar, oil, rice, and the like. Nigeria is one of the world's largest suppliers of oil; however, the price of the commodity is beyond the reach of common man. The price per gallon has increased over 1000 percent since 1999 when the present regime came to power. The rate of inflation is too high. Nigerian inflation is galloping, but the increase in money income is crawling. Real income is negative as most of the Nigerians, whatever their position in their establishment, are living below the poverty line. This is because being one's brother's keeper, one must help one's relatives who are hard up. Only the corrupt politicians spent money stolen from their people lavishly. Roads are death traps, and electricity is epileptic as power outage occurs more than 80 percent of the time in most Nigerian cities. The people resort to using generators, which created health hazards in a society where hospitals can best be described as mere consulting clinics for the lack of medicines and the dearth of doctors who have emigrated in search for greener pastures in America.

Most contemporary migrants can be categorized into the following:

a. The youths who are lured to America because of the bright light and promise of a better future. This group is running away from home because their future has been mortgaged by politicians who have nothing good, according to the youths, for the country.

b. The intellectuals who were forced out of the country because of lack of freedom and decline in economic fortune. The governments of African nations are suspicious of this group. Most of them are clamped into prison, and they were not given the freedom to do their work. They are poorly paid, and the whole structure in the academia is politicized. In fact, in Nigeria, the process of becoming a professor is affected by ethnicity and national politics. Some officers of universities are political representatives in those institutions, sent there to victimize the intellectuals so that they might not trouble the government. Most intellectuals who studied in America in particular had to return to work.

c. Those who are now benefiting from the Diversity Visa lottery. This is a mixed group, but they are mostly possessing middle-level education from high school or technical colleges. A significant percentage possesses the first degree. The youths detest the present political and economic structure of African nations, so they are those who are mostly attracted to the program.

Perception of Contemporary Black African Immigrants

African immigrants today are not as monolithic as their forerunners in the 1920s. Each of the groups has its unique behavior, leading to a meaning in the mind of the preceptor. However, there is a general consensus that the pre-1920s migrant made a better impression in the mind of their hosts than the present immigrants. The activities of the present immigrants have both the negative and positive dimensions.

Generally, the youths who came in search of bright lights were disappointed when they saw things in America were not as good as they were made to believe. This led to their behavior and attitudes, which gave them a negative perception in the USA. They therefore brought in different coping mechanisms, which include such objectionable things as cheating, stealing, Internet fraud, credit card offenses, and impersonation. They can do anything to make ends meet. Most of these are illegal. This class of immigrants mostly is illegally staying in the USA. Some came through a visitor's visa that had expired a long time ago, but they cannot go back home. This was based on the situation they left at home and their conditions in America. Most of the youths had borrowed and utilized their last savings to come to America. In fact, according to Arthur (2000), the USA was their last port of call. They have traveled via many countries in order to secure the visa to the USA. They have paid their last pennies to some middlemen who claimed the ability to secure foreign visas to intending migrants. Going back home will therefore be a failure, there will be no job, no money from any savings, and no relative to help them. Their relatives who had helped them initially when trying to migrate to USA believe they have invested and are waiting for the return on the investment when the migrant start sending money to him at home. Going back is, therefore, a real shame; the alternative for the migrant is to be playing the game of survival in America that, when negative, becomes illegal and dents his image before the host community. We are not saying that this picture is true of all African migrants. In fact, Okafor (2003) had noticed this earlier:

> *Obviously not every recent African immigrant has these problems, but every one can reflect on the problems . . . so as to be able to help those recent African immigrants who are trying to adjust to life in the USA.*

In a positive way, the youths are hardworking, and most of them show how one can make ends meet in the face of scarcity and uncertainties. They entered the area of jobs which they would have not liked to do in their countries. They easily changed their majors and professions. Most of the females have entered the nursing and social work professions. Some of them engage in doing more than two jobs a day with little or no time to rest.

Those who migrated in order to avoid conflict with the system or who came earlier but refused to go back are already very highly educated, as many of them possess the PhDs and are medical doctors and engineers. They are professors in the universities; some established their private businesses and worked in the hospitals. Their actions resemble those of the pre-1920s immigrants' but they did not have their kind of opportunities. The precolonial migrants came during the colonial period in Africa. They therefore had the sympathy of the African American population with whom they were fighting to liberate Africa and take the black population out of the inhuman position they were subjected to by the system. There was a kind of symbiotic relationship between them and the host black community. The new immigrants cannot enjoy such a relationship fully today. Although today there is cooperation between Africa and the African American community, such cooperation can only occur at an official level between the actor and the respective African nation's government. Africa is now politically free. The rulers are black Africans, and individual migrants can no longer hide under the guise of being a nationalist to elicit support from black Americans. Instead, this group of migrants is looked upon with suspicion by the African Americans. They look on them as coming to America to compete with them to take away the jobs and other opportunities due to the blacks in the USA. The relationship between them and the African Americans is not so much cordial at the informal level. At the formal level, the harshness is being mitigated by state laws that prohibit discrimination. Some African migrants in the teaching profession report that even students sometimes express the feelings of near hatred in the classes, especially if the professor expresses his dismay at some attitudes he considers not good enough on the part of the students. It was like the African Americans today are trying to show the migrants their displeasure on the roles played by the forefathers of the migrants in the slavery incidents of the eighteenth and nineteenth centuries. An appeal to the similarity in origin cannot save the situation, as most of African Americans are not much conversant with the history of their ancestor. The culture is also not the same again. Appeal to culture cannot help as the African migrants detest some of the attitudes of the African Americans with respect to sex, leisure, family life, and education.

The African immigrant is also not as lucky with the dominant group—the whites—in American society. He perceives the racial discrimination against the African American and does not like it. He sympathizes with the African American, but the African American seems to believe that he is a part of the African American problem. With the white community, he is being treated in the same manner the African American is being treated. Attempts by the African migrant to distance himself from the black American results in him being looked upon as more inferior. Arthur (2000) reported that some of the methods utilized by the black African immigrant is to emphasize his accent. But this earns him more problems, as he stands being unofficially rejected in some jobs because he will not communicate well. One of the complaints against most migrant professors by American students is related to their accents. African professors themselves get highly frustrated after noticing his well-prepared lectures are not well appreciated by his students because they cannot understand his accent. A job seeker once lamented that the search committee once asked him how he will successfully cope with the problem of students understanding his accent.

Impacts of the African Migrants in America Today

Whatever may be his experience, observations show that African migrants have impacts on the American society today. It was sad to note that the United States to which they migrated believes that they are burdens, but Nwachuku (2003) believes otherwise because

> *the Africans who left their countries have impacted the number of Black people in the United States . . . They brought in with them creative talents, especially Intellectuals that enhanced the contribution of Black people to human civilizations*

It has been documented that the symbiotic political relation witnessed in the colonial times is still noticeable and still being propelled by the African immigrants. Migrants from the various African countries form associations that present information about their nations to the American government and association. They form a very tight bond between their home countries and American interests. They even form themselves into lobby groups to protect the interests of their countries and America. They lobby the United States government to be interested in African and black affairs.

The present problem concerning April 2007 has been constantly brought to the notice of the American government by Nigerian migrants. The impacts of the "new American" (as these migrants from Africa are being referred to) can be felt most in the area of education. They can be found in most American colleges and universities. Some of them teach in elementary and high schools. They are mostly found in the historically black colleges and universities where they give themselves tasks to be accomplished. They serve as professors in any discipline and are not always interested in black studies. These educated African migrants in the universities propagate Afrocentric ideas to enhance development of African and African American personalities. They preach the idea that African Americans should empower themselves through increase in academic. This, they believe, more than anything else, will integrate them into the American society. Afrocentrism is not a racist idea as they propounded it. It is a tool for the empowerment of all blacks. Zizwe (2003) saw this as an important contribution of African intelligentsia, most of whom are immigrants in American society:

> *The roots of Afrocentrism are deep in the global experiences and initiatives of African intelligentsia . . . Regardless of their point of origin, they were united in their efforts to change the predominantly academic approach toward the study and presentation of African people.*

The major aim of this contribution is to propagate African ideas and methods of doing things. They are always propagating the course of African and African America development in the United States. It has been established that the African immigrant is the most educated out of all the immigrants in America. The 2000 census shows that 49 percent of them have at least a bachelor's degree. In propagating Afrocentrism, scholars study such important areas as the family, crime, and community-based self-help organizations.

Conclusions

This chapter has examined the issue of the black African immigrant in American community. We are not claiming to have exhausted possible discussions on this topic.

We are delighted to note that this topic, which attracted little or no attention before is now considered very topical in academic circles of this important nature. As earlier indicated in 1910, Peter Roberts believes that the African (black) immigrant in America did not constitute enough blocks of immigrants to be studied, and he therefore omitted them in his book **Immigrant Races in North America**.

However, eighty years later in 1993, the African immigrants' population is thought of as very important to the extent that a Ford Foundation grant was awarded to study them. The immigrant population has grown from about 33,000 in 1900 to over a million today.

The black African population should be seen as a distinctive group in American society. It is a fact that they blend with the African American in color, but there are substantial differences in their views of life, attitudes, and social organization. The African immigrant belongs to the group of new immigrants contributing their quota to the development of American society today. They are in a symbiotic relationship with the African American in the issue of social development and recognition in the society. This symbiotic relationship should be well harnessed for the development of the two groups. However, the special needs of the African immigrant should also be addressed, as there are some specific differences that still differentiate black African immigrant from the African Americans. This is found in the areas of culture relating to the family, inheritance, marriage, and the raising of their children. Specific exceptions should be granted to the African immigrant on the issue of raising their children. Most immigrants are not comfortable with the situation, which—if not well managed—produces children who are deviants. Africans love their children and always believe that they should do everything to protect their future. This, they believe, can only be done through discipline done through love. A situation granting too much freedom to the children may not augur well for them later in life. Sending parents to jail for spanking a child is culture shock for the average African. It also baffles him when the husband is removed from his house because of a mere argument with a wife. This society confuses African family behavior with battering and child abuse that is common in the society here. The African family is based on the idea of love and cooperation. The husband's duty is to defend the wife and children against outside aggression and care for them. A man is supposed to fight any outside aggression to the point of death.

In all, we are saying that the positive contribution of black Africans in the various ways discussed above will be well established if his culture is respected, as he will have a good rest of mind to do more. The negative behaviors will be minimized if this is taken care of as they will have more peace of mind to deal with their situations. We also advocate a closer relationship between the immigrants and the African Americans. This will enhance their educational and socioeconomic development.

REFERENCES

Aduwo, Akintunde. 1977. Speech at the opening ceremony of the International Cocoa Research Conference, University of Ibadan. Ibadan: Cocoa Research Institute.

Alao, J. A. *The Extension of Agricultural Innovations in Akeredolu Ale Social Development in Nigeria.* Ibadan: NISER.

Arthur, John A. 2000. *Invisible Sojourners African Immigrant Diaspora in the United States.* Praeger: Greenwoods.

Asante, Molefi. 1980. *Afrocentricity: The Theory of Social Change.* Buffalo, New York: Amulefi Publications.

Awolowo, Obafemi. 1947. *Path to Nigerian Freedom.* Faber & Faber.

———. 1968. *The Peoples' Republic.* Ibadan: Oxford University Press.

Azikiwe, Nnamdi. 1968. *Renascent African*. London: Frank Cass & Co. Ltd.

Babatunde, Emmanuel D. 2006. "Dysfunctionality: Case Study of Some West African Immigrants." In *Exploring the African American Experience*. Edited by Levi Nwachuku. Lincoln, Pennsylvania: Lincoln University Press.

Bannard, C. L. 1956. *The Functions of the Executive*. Harvard University Press.

Barn, T. and G. M. Stalker. 1961. *The Management of Innovation*. London: Tavistock.

Batten, T. R. 1974. *The Non-Directive Approach to Group and Community Development*. New York: Basic Books.

Blunden, J. 1991. "Mineral Resources" and "The Environment Impact of Mining Processing." In *Energy, Resources, and Environment*. Edited by J. Blunden and A. Reddish. Hodder & Stoughton.

Brown, S. 1990. "Humans and Their Environments: Changing Attitudes." In *Environment and Society*. Edited by J. Silvertown and P. Sarre. Hodder & Stoughton.

Buller, R. and M. Vaile. 1984. *Health and Health Services.* London: Rutledge and Regan Paul.

Burgess, Ernest W. "The Growth of the City: An Introduction to a Research Project." In *The City.* Edited by R. Park and W. Burgess.

Central Bank of Nigeria Annual Report: 87. 1981.

Chacko, Elizabeth. 2003. "Ethiopian Ethos and the Making of Ethnic Places in the Washington Metropolitan Area." *Journal of Cultural Geography* 20.

Chad Basin Development Authority, SCIP Handbook: 7.

Cohen, Abner. 1969. *Customs and Politics in Urban Africa: A Study of Hausa Migrants in Yoruba Towns.* Berkeley: University of California Press.

Cohen, Percy. 1968. *Modern Social Theory.* New York: Basic Books.

Comte, August. "Plan of the Scientific Operations Necessary for Reorganizing Society." In *On Intellectuals.* Edited by Philip Reif. Garden City, New York: Doubleday & Company Inc.

Conference on the State of Nigerian Economy, Benin. 1984.

Confino, Michael. "On Intellectuals and Intellectual Traditions in Eighteenth and Nineteenth Century Russia." In *Intellectuals and Tradition*. Edited by Eisenstadt and S. R. Graubard.

Conn, Patrick E. 1980. *Organization Theory and Decision*. Chicago Science Research Associates Inc.

Cort, R. P. 1963. *Communicating with Employees*. Complete Management Library Prentice Hall.

Crozier, M. 1964. *The Bureaucratic Phenomenon*. London: Tavistock.

Damachi, U. G. 1972. *Nigerian Modernization: The Colonial Legacy* New York University Press.

Davidson, Basil. 1995. *Africa in History*. New York: Simon & Schuster.

Davies, B. M. 1979. *Community Health Preventive Health and Social Services* 4th ed. London: Beriliere Tindal.

Davis, J. G. 1956. *The Biu Book*. Norla, Zaria.

Durkheim, Emile. 1964. *Division of Labor*. New York: The Tree Press.

Economic Journal 53. June–September 1943.

Essang, S. M. 1971. "The Impact of Marketing Boards on the Distribution of Cocoa Earning in Western Nigeria." Mimeo NISER Papers, March.

Ezera, Kalu. 1964. *Constitutional Development in Nigeria*. Cambridge: Cambridge University Press.

Federal Government of Nigeria. *Fourth National Development Plan*: 79.

Federal Ministry of Information. *Nigerian First National Development Plan: 1962–68*.

Federal Ministry of Information. 1970. *Nigeria Second National Development Plan, 1970–74*: 35–40. Lagos Government Printer.

Federal Republic of Nigeria. 1990. *First National Rolling Plan, 1990–1992*. Lagos: Federal Ministry of Budget and Planning.

Federal Republic of Nigeria. *First Progress Report on Third National Development Plan*: 31. Lagos.

Frank, Andre Gunder. 1967. *Capitalism and Underdevelopment in Latin America*. London and New York: Monthly Review Press.

Garfinkel, Harold. 1977. *Studies in Ethnomethodology*. New Jersey: Prentice Hall.

Gibbon, J. H. 1989. "Strategies for Energy Use." In *Scientific American*, September 1989: 86–93.

Ginsberg, P. 1972. *Fundamentals of Industrial Sociology.* Bombay.

Greene, O. 1991. "Tackling Global Warming." In *Global Environmental Issues.* Edited by P. M. Smith and K. Warr. Stoughton: Hodder.

Gutman, Herbert. 1976. *The Black Family in Slavery and Freedom.* New York Random House

Halberstam, David. 1973. *The Best and the Brightest.* Connecticut: Faucet Publications.

Hall, Richard. 1977. *Organizations: Structure and Process.*

Hall, Edward T. 1973. *Silent Language.* Garden City: Anchor Books.

Heydebrand, Wolf. 1977. "Organizational Contradictions in public Bureaucracies." *The Sociological Quarterly* 18.

Hobson, J. A. 1978. *Imperialism: A Study.* University of Michigan Press.

Holmes, P. F. 1980. "Future Prospects of Oil Industry in Nigeria." *Shell Bulletin (Lagos)*, January: 6.

Horkheimer, Max. 1977. *Knowledge and Human Interests.* New Jersey: Prentice Hall.

Idachaba, F. S. *Concept and Strategies of Integrated Rural Development: Lessons from Nigeria.* Food policy technical research paper 1. Food Policy Research Program. Department of Agriculture, Economic University of Ibadan.

Igbozurike, U. M. 1978. "An Evaluation of the Impact of Land Fragmentation on Agricultural Productivity." *Resources and Development in Africa.* Proceedings of the Regional Conference of the International Geographical Union. Edited by J. S. Oguntoyinbo, M. O. Fulani, and O. Areola. Lagos.

Ikechukwu, Raymond. 2011. Ethnic Politics in Nigeria: Constitutional Law and the Dilemma of Decision Making. *Malaysia Journal of Social Science* 7 (2).

Intellectuals and Traditions. 1973. New York: Humanity Press.

Jones-Quartey, K. A. B. 1965. *A Life of Azikiwe.* Baltimore: Penguin Books 1965.

Jucker-Fleetwood, Erin E. 1962. *Nigeria's Six-Year Development Plan.* Basel, Switzerland: Basel Centre for Economic and Financial Research.

Katz, R. and D. Kahn. *The Social Psychology of Organizations.*

Koontz, Harold, et al. 1980. *Management International: Students' Edition.* London, et al.: McGraw Hill International Book Company.

Kroeber, A. and Clyde Klukhohn. 1963. "Cultural: A Critical Review of Concepts and Definitions." Paper in *Peabody Review of American Archaeology and Ethnology.* Vintage edition. New York: Alfred A. Knopf.

Kuhn, Thomas. *The Structure of Scientific Revolution.* The University of Chicago Press 1970.

Kwame, Nkrumah. 1971. *Neo-Colonialism: The Last Stage of Imperialism.* London: Pavat Publications.

Lawrence, Peter and R. Lee. 1984. *Insight into Management.* Oxford: Oxford University Press.

Leow, K. S. and K. O. Ologe. 1981. "Rate of Soil Wash under a Savanna Climate: Zaria, Nigeria." Paper Presented at the Twenty-Fourth Annual Conference of the Nigerian Geographical Association, Kano.

Lloyd, P. C., ed. 1966. *The New Elite of Tropical Africa.* Oxford: Oxford University Press.

Lugard, F. D. 1922. *Dual Mandate for British Tropical Africa.* London: Lockwood.

Marris, Peter. 1961. *Family and Social changes in an African City.* London: Routledge and Kegan Paul.

Marx, Karl. *The German Ideology.*

———. 1967. "Historical Tendency of Capitalist Accumulation." In *Capital:* 761–774. Edited by F. Engels. New York: International Publishers.

———. *The Eighteenth Brumaire of Louis Napoleon.* Moscow: Progress Publishers, 1967.

Mazrui, Ali. 1978. *Political Values and the Educated Class in Africa.* Berkeley: University Of California Press.

McKee, J. B. 1981. *Sociology: The Study of Society.* New York: Holt, Rinehart, and Winston.

Millete, R. 1990. "West Indian Families in the US." In *Black Families.* Edited by H. Cheatham and J. Stewart.

Minitzberg, H. 1973. *The Nature of Management Work.* New York: Harper.

Moyniham, Daniel Patrick. 1960. *The Negro Family: The Case for National Action.* US Government Printing Office.

NEST. 1991. *Nigeria's Threatened Environment: A National Profile*. Ibadan: NEST.

Nisbet, Robert. 1977. *Social Change and History*: 6. London: Oxford University Press.

Nnoli, Okwudiba. 1981. *Path to Nigeria Development*. Cordesria.

———. 1989. *Ethnic Politics in Nigeria*. Fourth Dimension Press.

Nwachuku, Levi A. 2002. "Nnamdi Azikiwe and Lincoln University: An Analysis of Symbiotic Relationship." *Lincoln Journal Of Social and Political Thought* 1 (1).

———. 2006. "African American Studies: Significance and Meaning Revisited." In *Exploring the African American Experience*. Edited by Levi Nwachuku. Lincoln, Pennsylvania: Lincoln University Press.

———. 2006. "Africa and African Americans: The Future in Perspective." In *Exploring the African American Experience*. Edited by Levi Nwachuku. Lincoln, Pennsylvania: Lincoln University Press.

Nyerere, Julius. "The Arusha Declaration." In *Peasant and Peasant Society*.

Ogunnika, O. "Cash Crop and Problem of Food Shortage in Nigeria: Towards a Realistic Policy." Presented at ASUU.

————. 1985. "Institutional Innovations and Rural Development: A Study of CBDA in Borno." Presented at Second Annual Conference of NRSA, Oyo.

————. 1994. *Interethnic Tension Management in Nigeria: An Interpretative Approach.* Lagos: Mufets Nigeria.

————. 1998. "Interethnic Tension: Conflict and Control in Nigerian Cities." *International Journal of Politics Culture and Society* 1 (4).

Ogunnika, Olu. 1982. "American Managers in Alien Lands: Analysis of the Cultural Environment of Business." MBA thesis. New York: New York Institute of Technology.

————. 1994. "Communication Distortion in the Nigeria Press." *Sahel Analyst* I.

Okafor, Lawrence A. 2003. *Recent Immigrants to the USA: Their Concerns and How Everyone Can Succeed.* Pittsburg: Rosedog Books.

Okafor S. O. 1970. *Indirect Rule in Nigeria.* Oxford: Oxford University Press.

Okoli, P. U. U. 1991. "Edited the Nigerian Environment; Non- government Action Ibadan Peter. 1961. Publication.

Olatunbosun, Dupe. *Nigeria's Neglected Rural Majority.* Ibadan: Oxford University Press.

Olatunde, Oloko. 1981. Inaugural lecture at University of Lagos.

Olayide, O. (19) "Agricultural Technology and Nigerian Small Farmers" In *Nigerian Small Farmers.* CARD: University of Ibadan, Nigeria.

———.1976. *Issues in Development of Tropical Africa*: 2. Ibadan: University of Ibadan Press.

Olayide, S. O. 1989. "Agricultural Policy of the Military Era, 1966–79." In *The Nigerian Economy Under the Military.* Proceedings of the 1980 Annual Conference of the Nigerian Economic Society, Zaria.

Our Common Future *Explained.* 1991. London IIED and Earth Scan Publication Ltd.

Parker S. R., et al. 1981. *The Sociology of Industry.* London: George Alton & Unwind Ltd.

Paths to Nigerian Freedom. 1938. Faber & Faber.

Park, Robert. 1974. "The City: Suggestion for investigating behavior in Urban Environment." In *The City*: 1–46. Robert Park and N. Burgess. Chicago and London: University of Chicago Press.

Poe, D. Zizwe. 2006. "Introduction to Afrocentric Thought." In *Exploring the African American Experience*. Edited by Levi Nwachuku. Lincoln, Pennsylvania: Lincoln University Press.

Rockwell, Susanne. 2003. "Jacob Oluponna Studies African Migration in America." *Dateline UC Davis*, January 31.

Rodney, Walter. 1982. *How Europe Underdeveloped Africa*. Enugu: Ikenga Publishers.

Rosenstein-Rodan, Paul N. *Problems of Industrialization of Eastern and Western Europe*.

Simon, I. G. 1990. "The Impact of Human Societies on Their Environment." In *Environment and Society*. Edited by J. Silvertown and P. Sarre. Hodder & Stoughton.

Smith P. M.1991. "Sustainable Development and Equity." In *Global Environment Issues*. Edited by P. M. Smith and K. Warr. Hodder & Stoughton.

Smyth H. H. and Mabel Smyth. 1960. *The New Nigerian Elite*. Stanford, California: Stanford University Press.

Szasz, Thomas. 1961. *The Myth of Mental Illness*. New York: Harper & Row.

Thompson, Moritz. 1969. *Living Poor: A Peace Corps Chronicle*. Seattle: University of Washington Press.

Titmuss, R. M. 1960. *Essays on the Welfare State*. London: George Allen and Unwin Ltd.

Van den Berghe, Pierre L. 1973. *Power and Privileges at an African University*. Cambridge, Massachusetts: Schenkwan Publishing Co. Inc.

Vidich A. J. and J. Bensman. *Small Town in Mass Society*.

Webber, Melvin M. "Planning in an Environment of Change." *Town Planning Review* 39 (3–4): 179–195 and 277–295. October 1968 and January 1969.

Weber, Max. 1971. *The Interpretation of Social Reality*. Edited by J. E. T. Eldridge. New York: Charles Scribner and Sons.

Williams, S. K. T. *Rural Development in Nigeria*. Ile-Ife: Ife University Press.

Wilson, William Julius. 1987. *The Truly Disadvantaged.* Chicago: University of Chicago Press.

Wolf, Eric. 1969. *Peasant Wars of the Twentieth Century.* New York: Harper & Row.

Zuvekas, C. 1979. *Economic Development: An Introduction.* USA: Macmillan.